CLASSIC ANIMAL STORIES

CLASSIC ANIMAL STORIES

Introduced by
GERALD DURRELL

HAMLYN

CONTENTS

Illustrations by: Victor Ambrus, Val Biro, Mike Codd (David Lewis Management), Gwen Green, Douglas Hall, Bob Hersey (Linden Artists), Terry Riley (McCall Marketing and Design), Terry Rogers (Linden Artists), Meg Rutherford.

Designed by Robert Mathias and Kit Johnson

Published in 1989 by
The Hamlyn Publishing Group Limited,
a division of Paul Hamlyn Publishing,
Michelin House, 81 Fulham Road, London SW3 6RB

ISBN 0 600 55733 2
Produced by Mandarin Offset
Printed and bound in Hong Kong

INTRODUCTION
BY
GERALD DURRELL

Before prehistoric man had learnt to write and to read, he was creating animal books. That is to say, he was producing picture books by painting the walls of the caves in which he lived, and most of these beautiful pictures generally depicted animals of one sort or another, some of them now, unfortunately, long since extinct. Animals were very important to primitive people, for they supplied them with food and clothing, and down through the ages, we have been acutely aware of the other animals that inhabit the planet with us. Since the invention of writing, it is interesting to note that there have probably been as many books written by human beings about the other animals in the world as there are books by human beings *about* human beings.

Words, as you know, are rather like bricks. With bricks you can build a cottage or a cathedral, a village or a huge town. Through the magic of words you can enter another person's mind, illuminate it with pictures and silently give that person your thoughts. So reading and writing, when they were invented, were the most important means of communication between people – and they still are today, in spite of TV and radio.

There are many different ways in which to write about animals. There is the straightforward scientific work that describes the biology of the animal; then there are books like *Ring of Bright Water* or *Born Free* which are histories of individual animals and their relationship with their human owners. Some of these make fascinating reading and teach us a great deal about our contact with the rest of the animal world. The description by Gavin Maxwell in *Ring of Bright Water* of the problems of dealing with a boisterous otter in a London studio is both beautifully written and very funny, although whether it would persuade you that an otter makes an ideal pet is quite another matter.

The other books about animals are anthropomorphic, in other words, the animals are given human characteristics. They speak and think like human beings, which is, of course, something no animal does in real life. They have their own methods of communication (sometimes very complex ones), but they do not, as far as we know, think exactly like humans. Nevertheless, these stories have a great charm of their own, for who has not had enormous pleasure from reading such books as *Winnie the Pooh* or *The Wind in the Willows*?

I hope you will find some of the stories in this collection equally enchanting. *Charlotte's Web*, for example, introduces us not only to Charlotte A. Cavatica the brainy and resourceful spider but also to Wilbur the pig, who is a wonderful character, a pig of considerable personality. Then there are the captivating cats in *The Mouse Butcher* and their extraordinary adventures. In this story the frightening description of the Great Mog would, I think, make even Frankenstein grow pale with alarm at the thought of meeting such a fearsome cat.

Another fascinating cat story is the tale of *Thomasina*, who was murdered, but it is also interesting because of the way that cat behaviour is described. I knew a man once who was allergic to cats, and if one came near him he would start to sneeze uncontrollably. Cats seemed in some mischievous way to sense this, and if one walked into a room full of people they would make a beeline for my unfortunate friend, and before he had noticed it, the cat would jump on his lap and start rubbing itself against him and off he would go into a great sneezing fit. The animal would ignore all the other people in the room and concentrate all its attentions on my poor friend. As you will find out, Thomasina had a similar sense of humour and used it to annoy the father of the little girl with whom she lived.

As you read these stories I am sure you will be amazed, as I am, not only by the descriptive powers of the authors, but their fabulous imaginations. Reading is the most wonderful thing in the world, for it allows you to use *your* imagination. It is rather like switching on a television set inside your head. As you begin *Charlotte's Web*, you will feel as wet as if you had been out in a thunderstorm, and in *Ring of Bright Water*, you will feel the pain Maxwell must have suffered when his otter bit right through his hand. When the Great White Whale in *Moby Dick* attacks the longboat, you will hear the scrunch and crackle of its teeth as it bites the boat in half. You can experience all these things without leaving your chair.

These are ten superb stories, beautifully written and I know you will want to read the books from which they came to complete your pleasure, if not to satisfy your curiosity as to what happens to their main characters, the animals.

Gerald Durrell

A KESTREL FOR A KNAVE

Little Billy Casper lives in the north of England in a community where money is tight and prospects are few. His family and friends are tough and Billy has had to learn how to survive. Billy's only love and joy is his kestrel which he has trained from the nest and about which he enthuses brightly and knowledgeably. One of his teachers, Mr Farthing, is sympathetic to his situation and tries to communicate with the boy.

HOME, STRAIGHT HOME, and straight down the garden to the shed. He looked between the bars, clicking his tongue. The hawk lobbed off her perch, and with one wing-flick reached the shelf behind the door. Billy tapped the bars, then hurried back up the path to the garage.

Inside, on a bench built across the back, was a round board with BREAD carved in relief round its perimeter. The wood was scrubbed white, and hundreds of knife cuts had criss-crossed the surface into tiny geometrical figures. Across the board lay a knife, its blade gleaming stainless, in contrast to the ground steel of its teeth. Two brass rivets secured the handle, which was as smooth and dead as driftwood. Beside the board lay a leather satchel, and a scrubbing brush, bristles up.

Billy lifted the flap of the satchel and took out a grease-proof paper packet. When he opened it a few pieces of beef were stuck to the paper like Elastoplast. He sniff-sniffed the beef, then placed it on the board and went outside.

He crossed to the kitchen door, unlocked it, and walked straight through the kitchen to the living-room. It was cold and quiet, and darkness shaded the corners. Articles of clothing littered the furniture, their shapes determined by the weight and textures of the materials; woollen clumps, cotton spreads and nylon slip slithering over one arm of the settee. On the table used crockery was grouped about the checked cloth like the pieces of an abandoned game. Billy knelt down and felt under the settee. He came up with an air rifle, then crossed to the fireplace and reached up to a Toby Jug, looking pleased with himself at one end of the mantelpiece. He was full of lead pellets. Billy tipped him up and a soft stream of lead poured out of the black hat into his palm. Then, as he was replacing the jug, he noticed the two half-crowns holding down a folded slip of paper next to the clock. The coins fitted perfectly, their bevelled edges corresponding to form one thick crown. He paused, his fingers still round the jug. Then he turned and walked away, stopped, and looked back at the mantelpiece. He broke the rifle open and fitted a slug, frowning and nibbling his bottom lip, and patting at the slug with his thumb long after it had snugged into position. A smear of grease stained the end of his thumb. He studied it, then lubricated the tip of his forefinger by rubbing finger and thumb together.

The gun was .22 calibre, fitted with telescopic sights.

'Right then, odds I take it, evens I don't.'

He raised the rifle and aimed at the clock, the hairlines of the sights dividing the face like a hot-cross bun. He panned across to the Toby

Jug, sighting the grin, the belly, the beer mug, then brought it back across to the money and squeezed the trigger. The top coin spun up as though tossed by a thumb, reaching its zenith as the bottom one bounced out of the hearth on to the rug, heads, while the top one rattled and settled on the mantelpiece. Re Re Re Re Rrrrrrrrrrr, tails, and the betting slip zig-zagged in ever increasing arcs out under the table. Billy ran across to discover his luck.

'Shit!'

He dropped the coins into his jacket pocket and crouched under the table for the betting slip. As he stood up he unfolded it:

5/-

DOUBLE: CRACKPOT
TELL HIM HE'S DEAD.
JH.

He refolded the slip and stuffed it into the same pocket as the money, then left the house and shut the door behind him. The noise made a starling fly off the gutter, making Billy glance up as he locked the door.

He entered the garage, opened the back window, the side window, then placed a stool over a chalk X, drawn in a position where he could see squarely through both windows by merely turning his head. He settled down on the stool to wait. Nothing happened. He sat with the rifle across his thighs, whistling softly and rocking his feet silently in tune. He stopped whistling and rocking when a house sparrow landed on top of the kestrel's hut. He crept to the back window. When he raised his head the sparrow had gone. So he crept back to his stool and settled again.

There was a continuous CHIP CHIP of sparrows, but the only ones in view were out of range specks on chimney turrets. Then a cock sparrow landed on the gutter above the back bedroom window. It stood on one leg and scratched its beak with a high speed shuttering of the other foot, roused its feathers and settled, its fluffed body curving up over the gutter like an egg in a cup. Billy slipped off his stool to the window and eased one eye round the frame. Still there. He lifted the rifle and slowly poked it out, angling and swivelling it in the sparrow's direction. The sparrow stopped chipping and looked about, its feathers slicking to its body, revealing its true thin shape. Billy froze. Pause. The sparrow relaxed, and continued its song, chip. chip. chip. Billy scroamed into a comfortable kneeling position, and, jacking his left elbow on the window ledge and steadying the barrel on the side of the frame, brought the sparrow into sight. A grey pom-pom with a black bib; a grey capped head turning in profile to silhouette the tiny beak splitting wide at each utterance. A well defined study, edged black against the slate background. Billy adjusted the sights just a shade to pinpoint the intersection of the hairlines on to the bib. Hold it. Squeeeeze. The kick back made him jump and blink and open both eyes in time to see the sparrow plumping head first wings out down the back-cloth of brick. Reloading the rifle he ran out to where the sparrow lay on the concrete. He touched it with the barrel-tip, then carefully turned it over. It lay still. So he

bent down and picked it up. Both eyes were closed. A thin line of blood emphasised the division of the beak, but there was no futher sign of violence. Billy scuffed the plumage on its breast, and fanned its wings to look underneath them. But there was no mark where the slug had entered. He smoothed the feathers and refolded the wings, then held the rifle out at arms length and fired it down into the soil near his feet. No earth flew, and there was no sign where the pellet had entered. Just the same still formation of sods and pocked earth.

He took the sparrow back into the garage, put it into the satchel, and took out the lure. He tied a scrap of beef to each side of it, then replaced it and checked the contents of the satchel; from pocket – penknife, whistle, creance; back pocket – swivel and leash, lure, sparrow – and beef scraps. He put the satchel on, took his gauntlet down from a nail above the bench and left the garage.

The hawk was waiting for him. As he unlocked the door she screamed and pressed her face to the bars. He selected the largest piece of beef, then, holding it firmly between finger and thumb with most of it concealed in his palm, he eased the door open and shoved his glove through the space. The hawk jumped on to his glove and attacked the meat. Billy swiftly followed his fist into the hut, secured the door behind him, and while the hawk was tearing at the fringe of beef, he attached her swivel and leash.

As soon as they got outside she looked up and tensed, feathers flat, eyes threatening. Billy stood still, whistling softly, waiting for her to relax and resume her feeding. Then he walked round the back of the hut and held her high over his head as he climbed carefully over the

fence. A tall hawthorn hedge bordered one side of the field, and the wind was strong and constant in the branches, but in the field it had been strained to a whisper. He reached the centre and unwound the leash from his glove, pulled it free of the swivel, then removed the swivel from the jesses and raised his fist. The hawk flapped her wings and fanned her tail, her claws still gripping the glove. Billy cast her off by nudging his glove upwards, and she banked away, completed a wide circuit then gained height rapidly, while he took the lure from his bag and unwound the line from the stick.

'Come on, Kes! Come on then!'

He whistled and swung the lure short-lined on a vertical plane. The hawk turned, saw it, and stopped. . . .

'Casper!'

He glanced involutarily across the field. Mr Farthing was climbing the fence and waving to him. The hawk grabbed the lure and Billy allowed her to take it to the ground.

'Bloody hell fire.'

He pegged the stick into the soil and stood up. Mr Farthing was tiptoeing towards him, concentrating on his passage through the grass. With his overcoat on, and his trousers pinched up, he looked like a day-tripper paddling at the seaside. Billy allowed him to get within thirty yards, then stopped him by raising one hand.

'You'll have to stop there, Sir.'

'I hope I'm not too late.'

'No, Sir, but you'll have to watch from there.'

'That's all right. If you think I'm too near I can go back to the fence.'

'No, you'll be all right there, as long as you stand still.'

'I won't breathe.'

He smiled and put his hands in his overcoat pockets. Billy crouched down and made in towards the hawk along the lure line. He offered her a scrap of beef, and she stepped off the lure on to his glove. He allowed her to take the beef, then he stood up and cast her off again. She wheeled away, high round the field. Billy plucked the stick from the ground and began to swing the lure. The hawk turned and stooped at it. Billy watched her as she descended, waiting for the right moment as she accelerated rapidly towards him. Now. He straightened his arm and lengthened the line, throwing the lure into her path and sweeping it before her in a downward arc, then twitching it up too steep for her attack, making her throw up, her impetus carrying her high into the air. She turned and stooped again. Billy presented the lure again. And again. Each time smoothly before

her, an inch before her so that the next wing-beat must catch it, or the next. Working the lure like a top matador his cape. Encouraging the hawk, making her stoop faster and harder, making Mr Farthing hold his breath at each stoop and near miss. Each time she made off Billy called her continually, then stopped in concentration as he timed his throw and leaned into the long drawing of the lure and the hawk in its wake, her eyes fixed, beak open, angling her body and adjusting her flight to any slight shift in speed or direction.

She tried a new tactic, and came in low, seeming to flit within a pocket of silence close to the ground. Billy flexed at the knees and flattened the plane of the swing, allowing the lengthening line to pay out before her.

'Come on, this time, Kes! This time!'

She shortened her stoop, and counter stoop, which increased the frequency of her attacks, and made Billy pivot, and whirl, and watch, but never lose control of the lure or its pursuer. Until finally the hawk sheered away and began to ring up high over the hawthorn hedge.

'Come on then, Kes! Once more! Last time!'

And she came, head first, wings closed, swooping down hurtling down, towards Billy, who waited, then lured her – WHOOSH – up, throwing up, ringing up, turning; and as she stooped again Billy twirled the lure and threw it high into her path. She caught it, and clutched it down to the ground.

He allowed her to take the remaining beef scrap from the lure, then took her up and attached the swivel and leash. She looked up sharply at a series of claps. Mr Farthing was applauding softly. Billy started towards him and they met half-way, the hawk fixing the stranger every second of their approach.

'Marvellous, Casper! Brilliant! That's one of the most exciting things I've ever seen!'

Billy blushed, and there was silence while they both looked at the hawk. The hawk looked back, her breast still heaving from her exertions.

'It's beautiful, isn't it? Do you know, this is the first time I've ever been really close to a hawk?'

He raised a hand towards it. The hawk pecked and clawed at it. He withdrew his hand quickly.

'Goodness! . . . It's not very friendly, is it?'

Billy smiled and stroked her breast, ruttling under her wings with his fingers.

'Seems all right with you though.'

'Only 'cos she thinks I'm not bothered.'

'What do you mean?'

'Well when she used to peck me I kept my finger there as though it didn't hurt. So after a bit she just packed it in.'

'That's good. I'd never have thought of that.'

'You'll notice I always keep my hands away from her claws though. You don't get used to them striking you.'

Mr Farthing looked at the yellow scaled shins, the four spanned toes, the steely claws gripping the gauntlet.

'No. I'll bet you don't.'

Billy produced the sparrow from his bag and pushed it up between the finger and thumb of his glove. The hawk immediately pinned it with one foot and with her beak began to pluck the feathers from its head. Plucking and tossing in bunches, left and right, sowing them to the wind. Baring a spot, then a patch of puckered pink skin. She nipped this skin and pulled, ripping a hole in it and revealing the pale shine of the skull, as fragile and delicately curved as one of the sparrow's own eggs. Scrunch. The shell crumpled, and the whole crown was torn away and swallowed at one gulp. Another bite and the head was gone; even the beak was swallowed, being first finely crushed into fragments. Billy eased the sparrow up between his fingers, revealing most of its body. The hawk lowered her head and began to pluck the breast and wings. The breast fluff puffed away like fairy clocks; the wing quills twirled to the ground like ash keys.

Occasionally the hawk shook her head, trying to dislodge feathers which had stuck to the blood on her beak. If this failed she scratched at them with her claws, the flickering points passing within fractions of her eyes, wincing as though half in enjoyment, half in pain, like someone having a good scratch at nettle rash.

She cleared most of the breast, then pierced the skin with her beak and tore it open, exposing beneath the wafer of breast meat the minute organs, coiled and compact, packed perfectly into the tiny frame. The hawk disturbed their composition by reaching inside and dragging the intestines out. They swung from her beak, with the stomach attached like a watch on a chain. Then she snuffled and gobbled them down in a slithering putty-coloured pile.

'Uh!'

'Full o' vitamins them, Sir.'

The liver, a purply-brown pad; the heart, a slippery pebble; leaving only the carcass, a mess of skin and bone and feathers, which the hawk pulled apart and devoured in pieces. Any bones which were too big to crush and swallow comfortably were flicked away; clean white fragments, precise miniatures, knobbled and hollowed and lost in the grass. Until only the legs remained. The hawk nibbled delicately at the thighs, stripping them of their last shred of meat, leaving only the tarsi and the feet, which she spat aside. All gone. She stood up and shook her head.

Mr Farthing followed Billy over the fence, round to the front of the shed, and watched through the bars while the hawk was being released inside. She flew straight to her perch, lowered her head and began to feake, using the wood as a strop for her beak. Then she stood up and roused herself. Billy opened the door and stepped aside for Mr Farthing to enter. He squeezed quickly inside and they stood side by side looking at the hawk, which had settled down on one foot, her other foot bunched up in her feathers.

'Keep lookin' away from her, Sir, they don't like being stared at, hawks.'

'Right.'

Mr Farthing glanced round at the whitewashed walls and ceiling, the fresh mutes on the clean shelves, the clean dry sand on the floor.

'You keep it nice and clean in here.'

'You have to. There's less chance of her gettin' sick then.'

'You think a lot about that bird, don't you?'

Billy looked up at him, all the way up to his eyes.

'Course I do. Wouldn't you if it wa' yours?'

Mr Farthing laughed quietly, once.

'Yes I suppose I would. You like wildlife, don't you, Billy?'

'Yes, Sir.'

'Have you ever kept any more birds before this one?'

'Stacks. Animals an' all. I had a young fox cub once, reared it an' let it go. It wa' a little blinder.'

'What birds have you kept?'

'All sorts, maggies, jackdaws; I had a young jay once; that wa' murder though, they're right hard to feed, an' it nearly died. I wouldn't have one again, they're best left to their mothers.'

'And which has been your favourite?'

Billy looked at Mr Farthing as though his mentality had suddenly deteriorated to that of an idiot.

'You what, Sir?'

'You mean the hawk?'

'T'others weren't in t'same street.'

'Why not? What's so special about this one?'

Billy bent down and scooped up a fistful of sand.

'I don't know right. It just is that's all.'

'What about magpies? They're handsome birds. And jays, they've got beautiful colours.'

'It's not only t'colours though, that's nowt.'

'What is it then?'

Billy allowed a trickle of sand out of his fist on to his left pump. The grains bounced off the rubber toe cap like a column of tap water exploding in the sink. He shook his head and shrugged his shoulder. Mr Farthing stepped forward and raised one hand.

'What I like about it is its shape; it's so beautifully proportioned. The neat head, the way the wings fold over on its back. Its tail, just the right length, and that down on the thighs, just like a pair of plus-fours.'

He modelled the hawk in the air, emphasising each point of description with corresponding sweeps and curves of his hands.

'It's the sort of thing you want to paint, or model in clay. Painting would be best I should think, you'd be able to get all those lovely brown markings in then.'

'It's when it's flying though, Sir, that's when it's got it over other birds, that's when it's at its best.'

'Yes I agree with you. Do you know, you can tell it's a good flyer just by looking at it sitting there.'

'It's 'cos it looks streamlined.'

'It's what I was saying about proportion, I think that's got something to do with it. There's a saying about racehorses that if they look good, they probably are good. I think the same applies here.'

'It does.'

'And yet there's something weird about it when it's flying.'

'You what, Sir? Hawks are t'best flyers there are.'

'I don't mean . . .'

'I'm not sayin' there isn't other good uns; look at swallows and swifts, an' peewits when they're tumblin' about in t'air. An' there's gulls an' all. I used to watch 'em for hours when we used to go away. It wa' t'best at Scarborough, where you could get on t'cliff top an' watch 'em. They're still not t'same though. Not to me anyroad.'

'I don't mean anything to do with the beauty of its flight, that's marvellous. I mean . . . well, when it flies there's something about it that makes you feel strange.'

'I think I know what you mean, Sir, you mean everything seems to go dead quiet.'

'That's it!'

His exclamation made the hawk jerk up and tense.

'Steady on Sir, you'll frighten her to death.'

Mr Farthing pointed two fingers at his temple and triggered his thumb.

'Sorry, I forgot.'

The hawk roused and settled again.

'It was just that you got it so right about the silence.'

'Other folks have noticed that an' all. I know a farmer, an' he says it's the same wi' owls. He says that he's seen 'em catchin' mice in his yard at night, an' that when they swoop down, you feel like poking your ears to make 'em pop because it goes that quiet.'

'Yes, that's right. That's how I felt, it's as though it was flying in a, . . . in a, . . . in a pocket of silence, that's it, a pocket of silence. That's strange, isn't it?'

'They're strange birds.'

'And this feeling, this silence, it must carry over. Have you noticed how quietly we're speaking? And how strange it sounded when I raised my voice. It was almost like shouting in a church.'

'It's 'cos they're nervous, Sir. You have to keep your voice down.'

'No, it's more than that. It's instinctive. It's a kind of respect.'

'I know, Sir. That's why it makes me mad when I take her out and I'll hear somebody say, "Look there's Billy Casper there wi' his pet hawk." I could shout at 'em; it's not a pet, Sir, hawks are not pets. Or when folks stop me and say, "Is it tame?" Is it heck tame, it's trained that's all. It's fierce, an' it's wild, an' it's not bothered about anybody, not even about me right. And that's why it's great.'

'A lot of people wouldn't understand that sentiment though, they like pets they can make friends with; make a fuss of, cuddle a bit, boss a bit; don't you agree?'

'Ye', I suppose so. I'm not bothered about that though. I'd sooner have her, just to look at her, an' fly her. That's enough for me. They can keep their rabbits an' their cats an' their talkin' budgies, they're rubbish compared wi' her.'

Mr Farthing glanced down at Billy, who was staring at the hawk, breathing rapidly.

'Yes, I think you're right; they probably are.'

'Do you know, Sir, I feel as though she's doin' me a favour just lettin' me stand here.'

'Yes, I know what you mean. It's funny, though, when you try to analyse it, exactly what it is about it. For example, it's not its size is it?'

'No, Sir.'

'And it doesn's look terribly fearsome; in fact there are moments when it looks positively babyish. So what is it then?'

'I don't know.'

Mr Farthing moulded a fender of sand with the toe of one shoe, then slowly looked up at the hawk.

'I think it's a kind of pride, and as you say independence. It's like an awareness, a satisfaction with its own beauty and prowess. It seems to look you straight in the eye and say, "Who the hell are you anyway?" It reminds me of that poem by Lawrence. "If men were as

much men as lizards are lizards, they'd be worth looking at." It just seems proud to be itself.'

'Yes, Sir'

They stood silent for a minute, then Mr Farthing pushed his overcoat and jacket sleeves up to look at the time. The watch face was concealed under his shirt cuff. He revealed the face by lifting the cuff and sliding the strap down his wrist.

'Good lord! Look at the time, it's twenty past one. We'd better be off.'

He fumbled for the door fastener and backed out of the shed.

'I'll give you a lift if you like. I'm in the car.'

Billy blushed and shook his head. Mr Farthing smiled in at him through the bars.

'What's the matter, wouldn't it do your reputation any good to be seen travelling with a teacher?'

'It's not that, Sir . . . I've one or two things to do first.'

'Please yourself then. But you're going to have to look sharp, or you'll be late.'

'I know. I'll not be long.'

'Right. I'll be off then.'

His face disappeared from the bars, and reappeared a few seconds later.

'And thanks for the display, I really enjoyed it. You're an expert, lad.'

His face disappeared again, and for a few moments his barred charcoal back blocked the whole square. Then light, and other shapes like jigsaw pieces, grew round his receding silhouette, the house, the garage, the garden.

A car engine bleated. Bleated again and caught. BRUM–BRUMMED to a climax, then hummed away on a rising pitch.

Billy looked down and began to guide an oblong furry pellet through the sand with one toe. There was a kink in the fading car sound, a pause like a missed heartbeat as it changed up to a softer tone, and the final fade.

Billy picked the pellet up and inspected it in his palm. It was the size of a blackbird's egg, charcoal coloured, and shining faintly as though lacquered. He rolled it around his hand awhile, sniffed it, then carefully crumbled it with his finger tips. Inside the lacquered crust the fur was a lighter shade of grey, snuff dry, and wrapped inside the fur were tiny bones, and a tiny skull, with sets of dot-size teeth dotted to its tiny jaws. Billy rubbed the fur to ash, and gently blew it away like chaff from grain, leaving only the bones and the skull in his palm. He placed the skull on the shelf behind the door, then began to push the bones around with his forefinger; aimlessly at first, then linking them into a triangle, which he immediately destroyed, then reformed as an angular C. He studied this letter, then tried to remould it, but he could only make a D, so he shuffled the bones until their formation was meaningless.

Selecting the longest bone, he pincered it, pin thin, between his forefinger and thumb. The pressure drained two small patches of his skin white; then the points punctured, and a spot of blood formed on his finger tip; followed by a second on his thumb. He frowned and squeezed. This made him close one eye and bite his lips. The bone remained intact. Billy opened the pincers, and it stuck up out of the skin of his thumb like a little standard. He turned his thumb over, nail upwards. The bone still stuck, so he pulled it out and snapped it. The crack made the hawk open its eyes. Billy dropped the bones and carefully ground them into the sand with his pumps. Only the skull remained. He turned it to face the bars, then quietly left the hut, locked up, and with a final glance at the hawk, walked away up the path.

Barry Hines

(b.1939)

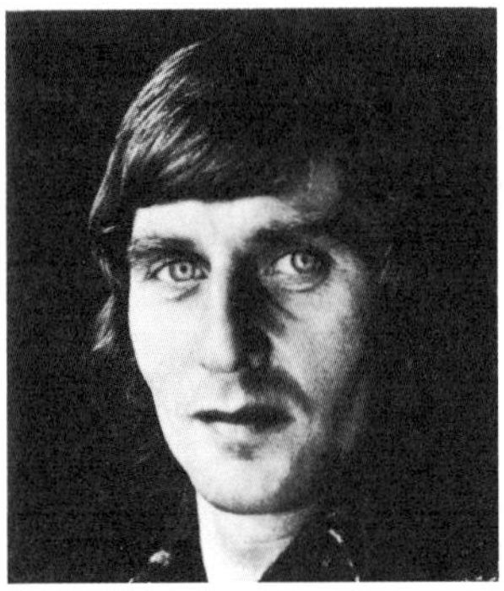

Barry Hines started his working life as a schoolteacher in Yorkshire and went on to teach at university. He has also been a teacher of creative writing, both in England and Australia. His own writings have included novels, television plays and screenplays for films.

RING OF BRIGHT WATER

Gavin Maxwell lives alone in a small cottage on the coast of the West Highlands of Scotland. After the death of his beloved dog, Jonnie, he begins to feel lonely in his isolated retreat. On a trip to southern Iraq, he acquires an otter, Chahala, which subsequently dies of food poisoning, but owning Chahala makes Maxwell realise an otter is the pet he wants. He is given Mijbil, and after an exhausting journey from Iraq, otter and owner arrive in London.

I LIVED AT THAT TIME in a studio flat near to Olympia, one large room with a sleeping gallery that opened on to the garage roof, and penthouse premises at the back containing kitchen, bathroom and box-room, each of diminutive size and resembling a divided corridor. Despite the absence of a garden, these unconventional premises held certain advantages for an otter, for the garage roof eliminated the normal difficulties of keeping a house-trained animal in a London flat, and the box-room opening from the bathroom provided quarters in which at any time he might be left for short periods with all his essential requirements. But just how short these periods would be – a maximum of four or five hours – had never struck me until Mij had already become the centre point round which, eccentrically, revolved my life. Otters that have been reared by human beings demand human company, much affection, and constant co-operative play; without these things they quickly become unhappy, and for the most part they are tiresome in direct ratio to their discontent. They can be trying, too, out of sheer inquisitiveness and exuberance of spirits, but not in the seemingly calculated way that is born of deprivation.

The spacious tile-floored bedroom of the Consulate-General at Basra, with its minimum of inessential furniture or bric-à-brac, had done little to prepare me for the problems that my crowded and vulnerable studio would present in relation to Mijbil. Exhausted as he was that first night, he had not been out of his box for five minutes before he set out with terrifying enthusiasm to explore his new quarters. I had gone to the kitchen to find fish for him, expected by prearrangement with my charlady, but I had hardly got there before I heard the first crash of breaking china in the room behind me. The fish and the bath solved the problem temporarily, for when he had eaten he went wild with joy in the water and romped ecstatically for a full half hour, but it was clear that the flat would require considerable alteration if it was to remain a home for both of us. Meanwhile sleep seemed long overdue, and I saw only one solution; I laid a sleeping bag on the sofa, and anchored Mij to the sofa-leg by his lead.

I have never been able fully to make up my mind whether certain aspects of otter behaviour merely chance to resemble that of human beings, or whether, in the case of animals as young at Mij was, there is actual mimicry of the human foster parent. Mij, anyway, seemed to regard me closely as I composed myself on my back with a cushion under my head; then, with a confiding air of knowing exactly what to do, he clambered up beside me and worked his body down into the sleeping-bag until he lay flat on his back inside it with his head on the

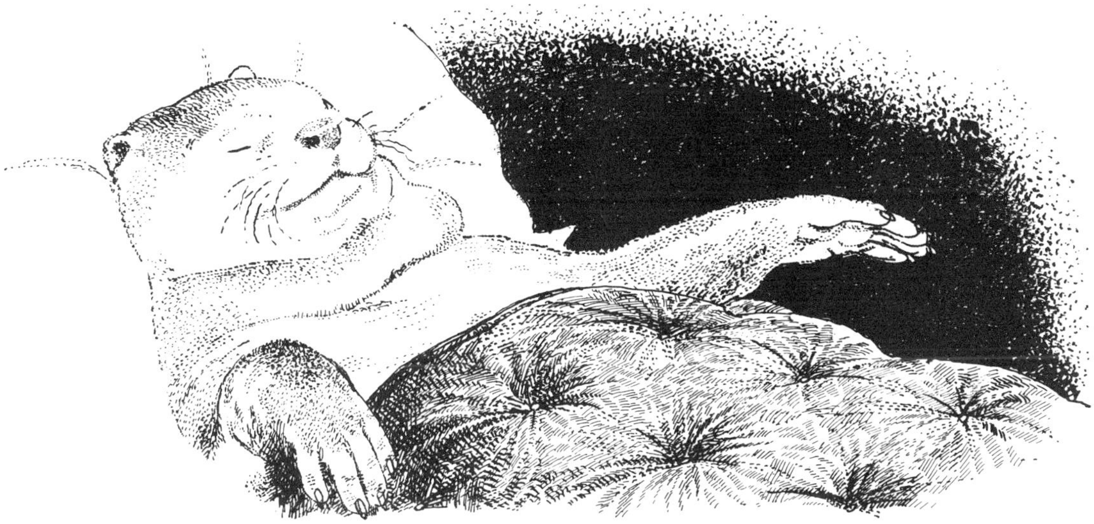

cushion beside mine and his fore-paws in the air. In this position, such an attitude as a child devises for its teddy-bear in bed, Mij heaved an enormous sigh and was instantly asleep.

There is, in fact, much about otters that encourages humans to a facile anthropomorphizing. A dry otter at play is an animal that might have been specifically designed to please a child; they look like 'invented' animals, and are really much more like Giovannetti's 'Max' than anything else, a comparison that has instantly struck many people upon seeing my otters for the first time – the same short legs, the same tubby, furry torso, vast whiskers, and clownish good humour. In the water they take on quite a different aspect and personality, supple as an eel, fast as lightning, and graceful as a ballet dancer, but very few people have watched them for long below the surface, and I have yet to see a zoo that gives its otters a glass-sided tank – a spectacle that I believe would steal the show from the whole aquarium.

Mij and I remained in London for nearly a month, while, as my landlord put it, the studio came to look like a cross between a monkey-house and a furniture repository. The garage roof was fenced in, and a wire gate fitted to the gallery stairs, so that he could occasionally be excluded from the studio itself; the upstairs telephone was enclosed in a box (whose fastening he early learned to undo); my dressing-table was cut off from him by a wire flap hinging from the ceiling, and the electric light wires were enclosed in tunnels of hardboard that gave the place the appearance of a power-house.

All these precautions were entirely necessary, for if Mij thought that he had been excluded for too long, more especially from visitors whose acquaintance he wished to make, he would set about laying waste with extraordinary invention. No amount of forethought that I could muster was ever able to forestall his genius; there was always something that I had overlooked, something that could be made to speak with a crash for his mood of frustration, and it did not take me long to learn that prophylaxis was more convenient than treatment.

There was nothing haphazard about the demonstrations he planned; into them went all the patience and ingenuity of his remarkable brain and all the agility of his muscular little body. One evening, for example, after the contractors had departed for the third of fourth time, leaving, as I thought, an otter-proof situation at last, I had confined Mij to the gallery for an hour in deference to the wishes of a female visitor who feared for her nylons. He appeared, after a few moments, balancing adroitly on the top of the gallery railing, paying no attention either to us or to the formidable drop below him, for his plan was evidently already mature. At various points along the length of this railing were suspended certain decorative objects, a Cretan shepherd's bag, a dagger, and other things whose identity now eludes me. Purposefully, and with an air of enormous self-satisfaction, Mij began to chew through the cords from which these *objets d'art* or *de voyage* hung. After each severance he would pause to watch his victim crash to the parquet floor below, then he would carefully renew his precarious, straddling progress along the rail until he reached the next. We stood, my visitor and I, waiting to catch the more fragile items as they fell, and I remember that when the last fruit, as it were, had fallen from the bough, she turned to me with a sigh and said, 'Don't you ever feel that this just simply can't go on?'

More usually, however, when he was loose in the studio, he would play for hours at a time with what soon became an established selection of toys, ping-pong balls, marbles, india-rubber fruit, and a terrapin shell that I had brought back from his native marshes. The smaller among these objects he became adept at throwing right across the room with a flick of his head, and with a ping-pong ball he invented a game of his own which would keep him engrossed for up to half an hour at a time. An expanding suitcase that I had taken to Iraq had become damaged on the journey home, so that the lid, when closed, remained at a slope from one end to the other. Mij discovered that if he placed the ball on the high end it would run down the length of the suitcase unaided. He would dash round to the other end to ambush its arrival, hide from it, crouching, to spring up and take it by

surprise as it reached the drop to the floor, grab it and trot off with it to the high end once more.

These games were adequate for perhaps half of all the time he spent indoors and awake, but several times a day he needed, as much psychologically as physically, I think, a prolonged romp with a human playmate. Tunnelling under the carpet and effecting to believe himself thus rendered invisible, he would shoot out with a squeak of triumph if a foot passed within range; or he would dive inside the loose cover of the sofa and play tigers from behind it; or he would simply lay siege to one's person as a puppy does, bouncing around one in a frenzy of excited chirps and squeaks and launching a series of tip-and-run raids. It was the 'tip' that was the trouble, for his teeth were like needles, and however gently he might try to use them, such games used, I am bound to say, to end with a certain amount of visible proof of his success in tactics left on the human hand. It did not hurt, but it made a bad impression upon visitors, many of whom were ready in any case to accord him the distrust appropriate to an alien upstart.

But I soon found an infallible way to distract his attention if he became too excitable, a way whose success was, I think, due to the refusal to be baffled by obstacles that is an otter characteristic. I would take the terrapin shell, wrap it in a towel, and knot the loose ends tightly across. He came to know these preparations, and would wait absolutely motionless until I handed him the bundle; then he would straddle it with his fore-arms, sink his teeth in the knots, and begin to hump and shuffle round the room in a deceptively aimless-seeming manner. Deceptive, because no matter how complex the

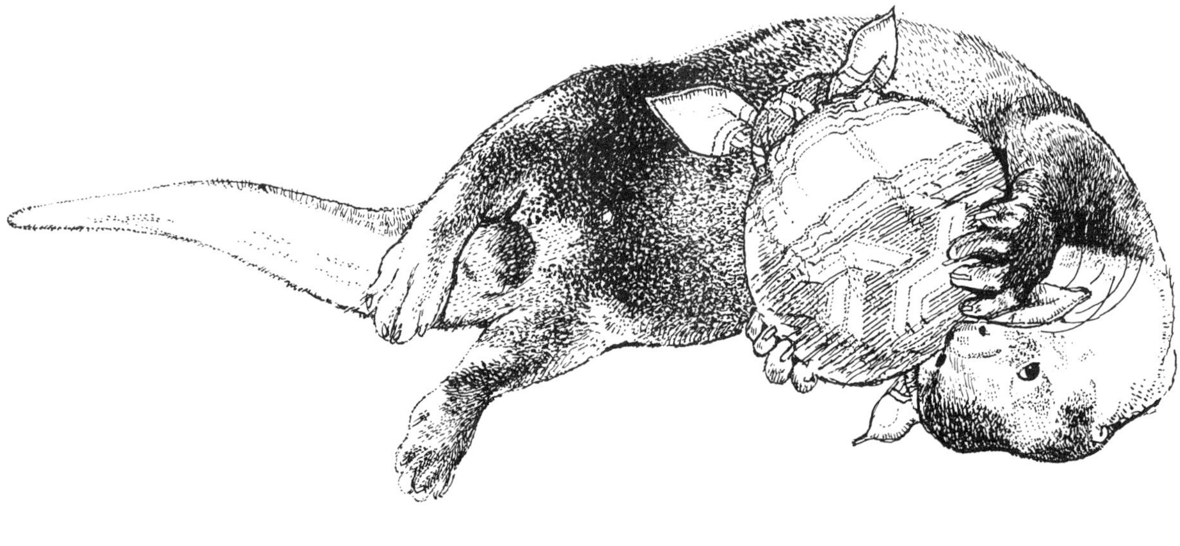

knots he would have them all undone in five or ten minutes. At the end of this performance he liked, and seemed to expect, applause, and he would then bring the towel and the terrapin shell to be tied up again. He brought the towel first, dragging it, and then made a second trip for the terrapin, shuffling it in front of him down the room like a football.

At night he slept in my bed, still, at this time, on his back with his head on the pillow, and in the morning he shared my bath. With utter indifference to temperature he would plunge ahead of me into water still too hot for me to enter, and while I shaved he would swim round me playing with the soapsuds or with various celluloid and rubber ducks and ships that had begun to accumulate in my bathroom as they do in a child's.

Outside the house I exercised him on a lead, precisely as if he had been a dog, and, like a dog, he soon showed preference for certain streets and certain corners at which dogs of all sorts and sizes had left stimulating messages that were, perhaps, the more fascinating for being, as it were, in a foreign language. Whether or not he could decipher their purport, whether or not they conjured up for him the various erotic, impudent or pugnacious images intended, he would spend minutes at a time sniffing these clearing-houses of local canine information, and would occasionally add to them some liquid comment of his own, tantalizingly cryptic, no doubt, to the next comer.

I was too timid of the result to allow him to meet any dogs so to speak nose to nose, and I would pick him up if we met unattended dogs in the street, but for his part he seemed largely indifferent to them. The only time that I was conscious of some mutual recognition taking place, some awareness of similarity between canine and lutrine values, was one morning when, setting out for his walk, he refused to be parted from a new toy, a large rubber ball painted in gaudy segments. This ball was too big for his mouth, so that he could only carry it sticking out from one side of his jaws like a gigantic gum boil, and thus encumbered he set off briskly up the street, tugging at his lead. Rounding the first street corner we came face to face with a very fat spaniel, unattended and sedately carrying in its mouth a bundle of newspapers. The respective loads of otter and dog made it difficult for either of them to turn its head far as as they came abreast, but their eyes rolled sideways with what appeared to me a wild surmise, and when they were a few paces past each other both suddenly stopped dead for a moment, as though arrested by some momentary mental revelation.

Mij quickly developed certain compulsive habits on these walks in the London streets, akin, clearly, to the rituals of children who on their way to and from school must place their feet squarely on the centre of each paving block; must touch every seventh upright of the iron railings, or pass to the outside of every second lamp post. Opposite to my flat was a single-storied primary school, along whose frontage ran a low wall some two feet high separating a corridor-width strip of garden from the road. On his way home, but never on his way out, Mij would tug me in the direction of this wall, jump up on it, and gallop the full length of its thirty yards, to the hopeless distraction both of pupils and of staff within. There was more than one street of which he would use one pavement only, refusing with dug-in toes to be led to the other side, and there were certain drain grilles through which he would peer motionless for long seconds before he could be led away from them. On return to the flat he would scrabble frantically to be let in, and the moment his lead was unhitched he would roll on his back and squirm with eye-bewildering speed and vigour before returning to his toys.

Many of his actions, indeed, appeared ritual, and I think that comparatively few people who keep wild creatures realize the enormous security-value of routine in the maintenance of an animal's contentment. As soon as routine is broken a new element enters, in however minute and unrecognizable a trace – the fear of the unknown which is basic to the behaviour of all animals, including man. Every living creature exists by a routine of some kind; the small rituals of that routine are the landmarks, the boundaries of security,

the reassuring walls that exclude a *horror vacui*; thus, in our own species, after some tempest of the spirit in which the landmarks seem to have been swept away, a man will reach out tentatively in mental darkness to feel the walls, to assure himself that they still stand where they stood – a necessary gesture, for the walls are of his own building, without universal reality, and what man makes he may destroy. To an animal these landmarks are of even greater importance, for once removed from its natural surroundings, its ecological norm, comparatively little of what the senses perceive can be comprehended in function or potentiality, and the true conditions for insecurity are already established. As among human beings, animal insecurity may manifest itself as aggression or timidity, ill-temper or ill-health, or as excessive affection for a parental figure; unfortunately this last aspect encourages many to cultivate insecurity in their charges, child or animal, as a means to an end.

It was about this time that Mij delivered his first serious, intentional, bite. He was fed now upon live eels – which I had learned to be the staple food of many races of otter – supplemented by a mixture of raw egg and unpolished rice, a sticky concoction for which he evinced a gusto no doubt influenced by his early life among the Arabs. The eels I kept in a perforated bucket under the kitchen tap, and fed them to him in the bath; it had become an established way of quieting him when he was obstreperous, to shut him in with a full bath of water and three or four eels. On this occasion I had closed the bathroom door imperfectly, and Mij elected to bring his second eel through and eat it in the studio. To this, though he was sodden with

water and the eel very slimy, there seemed no alternative, for it is folly to try to take away from a wild animal its natural prey; but when after a few mouthfuls he decided to carry it upstairs to the gallery I determined to call a halt, visualizing a soaking and eel-slimed bed. I put on three pairs of gloves, the outermost being a pair of heavily-padded flying gauntlets. I caught up with him half-way up the stairway; he laid down the eel, put a paw on it, and hummed at me, a high continuous hum that could break out into a wail. Full of euphoric self-confidence I talked away quietly to him, telling him that he couldn't possibly hurt me and that I was going to take the eel back to the bathroom. The humming became much louder. I bent down and put my heavily-gloved hand upon the eel. He screamed at me, but still he took no action. Then, as I began to lift it, he bit. He bit just once and let go; the canines of his upper and lower jaws passed through the three layers of glove, through the skin, through muscle and bone, and met in the middle of my hand with an audible crunch. He let go almost in the same instant, and rolled on his back squirming with apology. I still held the eel; I carried it back to the bath, where he refused to pay any further attention to it, fussing round me and over me and muzzling me with little squeals of affection and apparent solicitude.

There were two small bones broken in my hand, and for a week it was the size of a boxing glove, very painful, and an acute embarrassment to me in the presence of those who from the first had been sceptical of Mij's domesticity. I had been given a sharp and necessary reminder that though he might carry painted rubber balls through the London streets he was not a spaniel.

It was not lack of curiosity, so much as lack of time and opportunity, that made me delay for nearly three weeks before making any real effort to establish Mij's identity. It would, I thought, require a day's research in the library of the Zoological Society, and at that early stage Mij could not be left alone for more than an hour or so without fretting. But, as may be imagined, he caused no small stir in his walks through the streets of West Kensington, and it was increasingly borne in upon me that I could answer only in the most perfunctory and unsatisfactory terms the fire of questions with which our strolls were punctuated.

It is not, I suppose, in any way strange that the average Londoner should not recognize an otter, but the variety of guesses as to what kind of animal this might be came as no less of a surprise to me than the consistent accuracy with which a minority bracketed the bull's-eye without once touching it. Otters belong to a comparatively small group of animals called Mustellines, shared by the badger, mongoose, weasel, stoat, polecat, marten, mink and others; the official at Cairo airport had set an early precedent of outer scoring when he asked whether Mij was an ermine – which is, of course, a stoat in winter coat. Now, in the London streets, I faced a continual barrage of conjectural questions that sprayed all the Mustellines but the otter; wilder, more random fire hit on practically everything from 'a baby seal' to a squirrel. The seal heresy had deep root, and was perhaps the commonest of them all, though far from being the most bizarre; 'Is that a walrus, mister?' reduced me to giggles outside Harrods, and 'a

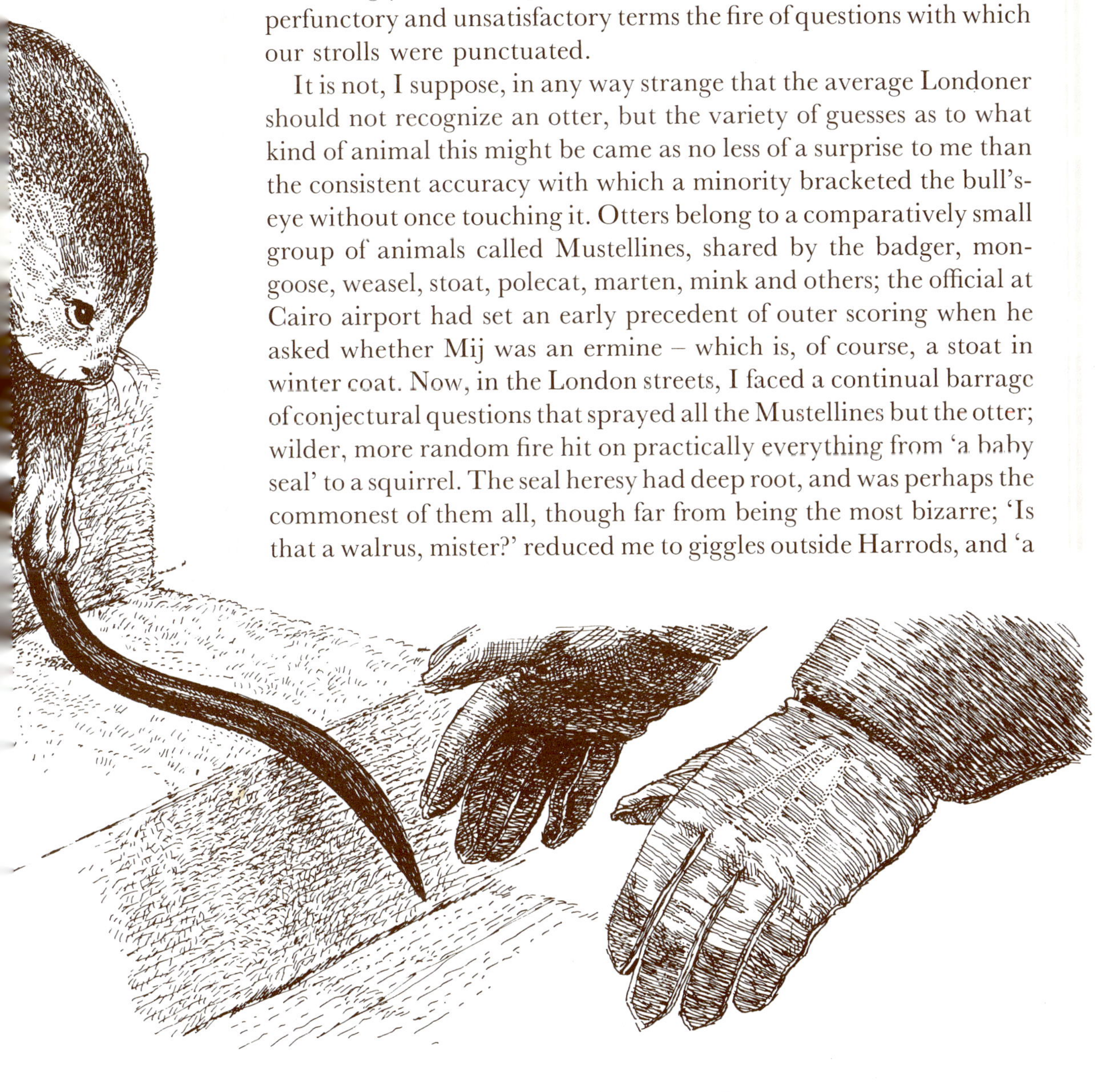

hippo' made my day outside Cruft's Dog Show. A beaver, a bear cub, a newt, a leopard – one, apparently, that had changed his spots – even, with heaven knows what dim recollections of schoolroom science and a bewildering latinized world of sub-human creatures – a 'brontosaur'; Mij was anything but an otter.

But the question for which I awarded the highest score – a question evading with contemptuous dexterity any possible inaccuracy on the part of the speaker; putting the blame, as it were, for the creature's unfamiliarity squarely on my own shoulders; hinting, or doing more than hint, that someone had blundered, that the hand of the potter had shaken; containing, too, an accusation of unfinished work unfit for exhibition – came from a Herculean labourer engaged, mightily

and alone, upon digging a hole in the street. I was still far from him when he laid down his pick, put his hands on his hips and began to stare. As I drew nearer I saw that this stare held an outraged quality, one of surprise, certainly, but also of affront, as though he would have me know that he was not one upon whom to play jokes. I came abreast of him; he spat, glared, and then growled out, 'Ere, mister – *what is that supposed to be?*'

It was, I think, his question more than any other that reminded me of my own ignorance; I did not, in fact, know what Mij was supposed to be. I knew, certainly, that he was an otter, but I also knew that he must be one of a species which, if known to the scientific world, was at least not known to live in the delta marshes of the Tigris and Euphrates, for the scant zoological literature that had accompanied me to Iraq made it plain that the only known otter of the Mesopotamian marshes was the Persian sub-species of the common European otter, *Lutra lutra*. Chahala, the cub that had died, had clearly belonged to that race; she had longer fur with 'guard hairs' in place of Mij's sleek, darker velvet; she was lighter on her throat and belly than upon her back, whereas Mij's body seemed to have been slipped into an evenly-dyed plush bag; the under side of her tail was not, as was Mij's, flat like a ruler.

In a village of the marshes between the Tigris and the Persian frontier I had bought two otter skins from the householder with whom we had been staying; both were, apart from any possible scientific interest, objects of fascination, for they had been 'case' skinned, the whole carcase having been removed, without a single incision, through the mouth. One of these skins belonged to Chahala's race; the other, contrast heightened by juxtaposition, was plainly of Mij's, a much larger and darker creature, whose fur was short and shiny and the colour of milkless chocolate. These two skins now reposed in my flat, pregnant with possibility and as yet unexamined by competent authority.

I telephoned to the Natural History department of the British Museum, in Cromwell Road, and the same afternoon Mr Robert Hayman arrived at my flat to examine the two skins and the living specimen. There is in the serious zoological world a dead-pan-ness, an unwillingness for committal, that must rival the most cautious of consulting physicians. Hayman was far too competent a zoologist, far too encyclopedic in his knowledge, to have been unaware in those first moments that he was looking at a skin and a living animal from a habitat that made the race quite unfamiliar to him, but he did not betray it. He took such measurements as Mij would permit, examined him closely, peered at his formidable array of teeth, and left bearing the two skins for comparison with museum series.

But in due course, after the slow, precise, painstaking processes of the taxonomic world, Mij's new race was proclaimed. Hayman summoned me to the museum to see the cabinets of otter skins from all over Asia, where the larger of mine lay, unlabelled and conspicuously differing from any other, in a drawer by itself, but in apposition to its nearest relatives. These, various sub-species of *Lutrogale*, a short-coated otter with a flat under side to the tail, ranged over most of Eastern Asia; according to their geographical race they were of a variety of hues from pale sandy to medium brown, but none had been recorded west of Sind, in India, and none resembled my specimens in colour.

There are very few people, and even fewer amateur zoologists, who stumble upon a sizeable mammal previously unknown to science; in the nursery world of picture-books of birds and beasts the few who had given their own names to species – Steller's Eider and Sea Eagle, Sharpe's Crow, Humboldt's Woolly Monkey, Meinerzthagen's Forest Hog, Ross's Snow Goose, Grant's Gazelle, Père David's Deer – had been surrounded for me with an aura of romance; they were the creators, partaking a little of the deity, who had contributed to the great panorama of bright living creatures in which, unshadowed and uncomplicated by knowledge, my childish fancy wandered. Now, when Hayman suggested that the new otter should bear my name, I experienced a sharp, brief conflict; I felt that it should bear his, for he, not I, had done the work; but something small and shrill from the nursery days was shouting inside me that I could be translated into the hierarchy of my early gods and wear, however perilously, the halo of a creator. ('Can I have it for my own?' we used to ask when we were small. 'For my *very* own?' Here, surely, was an animal that looked like it would always bear my name for ever and ever, unless some odious taxonomist of the future, some leveller, some jealous, dusty scribe of the backroom and the skeletons, were to plot against me and plan the destruction of my tiny, living memorial.)

So Mij and all his race became *Lutrogale perspicillata maxwelli*, and though he is now no more, and there is no ostensible proof that there is another living specimen in the world, I had realized a far-off childish fantasy, and there was a Maxwell's otter.

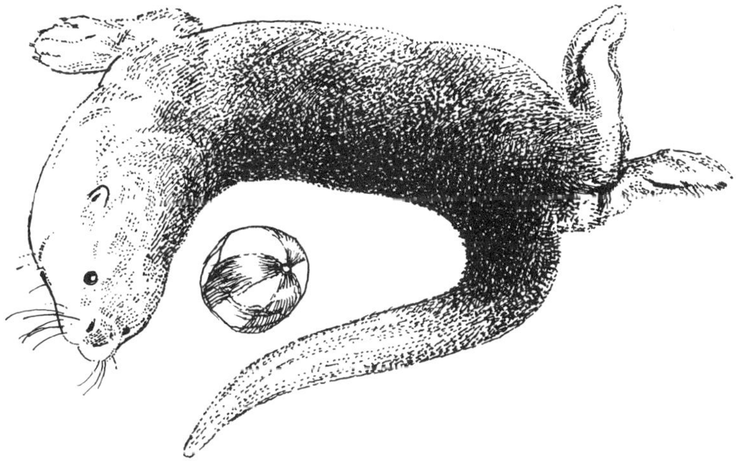

Gavin Maxwell

(1914–69)

Gavin Maxwell was a portrait painter as well as a writer. He was very much concerned with young people and with giving them the chance to explore the natural world which he himself loved so much. Gavin Maxwell was President of the British Junior Exploration Society, and also belonged to several societies which cared for wild creatures. One was the Wildfowl Trust and another, the Fauna Preservation Society. Several of Gavin Maxwell's books won awards and honours.

THOMASINA

Thomasina, the narrator of this story, is, by her own reckoning at least, a highly intelligent and beautiful ginger cat who is owned by Mary Ruadh, the young daughter of a lonely and embittered widower Andrew MacDhui, a small town vet. Just outside the town lives a young woman who is known as the Red Witch or Mad Lori. She has a great affinity with all animals and people who find MacDhui's ways cold and uncaring, often take their animals to her to be healed. The fates of Thomasina, the MacDhuis and Mad Lori are soon inextricably linked.

If it is family you go by, then you will certainly be impressed with mine, for I am a relative of that Jennie – Jennie Baldrin of Glasgow – about whose life and times and adventures in London, aboard ship and elsewhere, a whole book has been written and published.

We are Edinburgh on one side of my family, several of my forbears not only having been employed at the University in the usual capacity as hunters, but one or two are said to have contributed to scientific knowledge and advance. We are Glasgow on the other, the Jennie Baldrin side.

Jennie was my great-aunt and she was most distinguished and Egyptian-looking with a small, rather narrow head, long muzzle, slanting eyes and good-sized, rounded, well-upstanding ears, and in this I am said to resemble her closely, though, of course, our colouring is quite different. I mention this with excusable pride since it shows that we trace our ancestry back to the days when people had the good sense to recognise us as gods.

That false gods are worshipped today – well, more's the pity, for in Egypt, in the old days when members of our family were venerated in the temples, times were better and people, by and large, seemed happier. That, however, is neither here nor there and does not concern what I have to tell. Yet, if you know that once you were a god, no matter how long ago – well, it is bound to show somewhat in your demeanour.

Nor does Jennie play any part at all in what is to follow, except that I suppose I inherited something of her independence, courage and poise, not to mention elegance, and I brought in her name only as a possible point of interest to you should you happen to be familiar with her story.

I, too, have had a most curious adventure and experience, one of the most interesting and marvellous things that ever happened, at least that part which concerns myself.

I will not keep you in suspense. It has to do with a murder.

But what makes this story different from any you ever read is that the one who is murdered is – ME.

The name I bear, Thomasina, came about through one of those ridiculous and inexcusable errors committed by so many people who attempt to determine our sex when we are very young. I was originally christened Thomas when I came to live at the home of the MacDhuis in Glasgow to be the pet of Mary Ruadh, then aged three. When the error became obvious the name was simply feminised to Thomasina by Mrs McKenzie, our housekeeper, whether I liked it or not and without so much as a – by your leave.

I do not know why people are quite so stupid at determining our sex when we are young. The difference is easy enough to see if you will just *look* instead of guess, and take a little trouble, for with boys, things are apart, and with girls they are near together, and that's the rule, no matter how small they might be.

Mr Andrew MacDhui might have told at a glance, no doubt, since he was a veterinary surgeon. But he was a most queer man to follow the profession of doctor to animals, since he had little love for and no sentimental interest in them whatsoever, and hence never paid the slightest attention to me from the moment I came into the house, which I cannot say disturbed me. The disregard was mutual.

We lived in a large, rather gloomy house in Dunearn Street, which Mr MacDhui had inherited from his father, who was also a veterinary, when he died. The two lower floors were given over to the offices, surgery and animal hospital and we lived on the two upper ones, Mr MacDhui, his wife and Mary Ruadh. They all had red hair.

I have, too, or rather ginger coloured with a white blaze on my chest. But what people really seem to find irresistible about me is that I have four white feet, and the very tip of my tail is white to match. I am quite used to receiving compliments upon my looks and bearing.

Although I was then only six months old myself I remember Mary Ruadh's mother, Anne. She was beautiful and her hair was the colour of the copper pots by the fireside. She was very gay and always singing about the house which made it less dark and gloomy, even on rainy days. She was forever cuddling and spoiling Mary Ruadh and they would often spend time 'giving one another whispers' which was a kind of love-making. It was not an unhappy household in spite of Mr MacDhui. But it did not last long, for soon after I came Mrs MacDhui contracted a disease from a parrot that was being kept in the hospital and died.

That was a bad time for me, I can tell you, and if it had not been for Mrs McKenzie I do not know what would have happened to me, for Mr MacDhui half went out of his mind, they said, and it certainly sounded like it, the manner in which he raged and carried on, and the love he had had for his wife he now transferred to his daughter, and half frightened her to death with it, and me too, I can assure you. He kept staying away from home and would not go near his animal hospital for days on end and things were getting in a bad state when he received a visit from an old friend of his from the country, a minister by the name of Mr Peddie, and after that things got a little better and soon we had a great change.

It seems that Mr Peddie and Mr MacDhui had known one another when they were both students at Edinburgh University – they might even have known some of *my* family there – and Mr Peddie told Mr MacDhui that there was a practice for sale in the town where he lived and advised him to go there.

So, Mr MacDhui sold out his practice in Glasgow and the house on Dunearn Street where he was brought up and we all moved to Inveranoch on the west bank of Loch Fyne in Argyll where my tragedy happened to me.

Mary Ruadh then was six years old, going on for seven and we lived in the last house but one near the end of Argyll Lane. Our next-door neighbour was Mr MacDhui's friend, Mr Angus Peddie, the minister, who kept a most disgusting pug dog by the name of Fin. Ugh!

Our house was really two houses, one next to the other but separated and they were of white-washed stone with slate roofs; they were rather long and narrow, two stories high, with tall chimneys at each end on which there was usually perched a seagull. In one of these we lived and in the adjoining one was the office, waiting-room, surgery and hospital of Mr MacDhui. But, of course, we never went there for Mary Ruadh was forbidden to do so. After what had happened in Glasgow, Mr MacDhui had sworn he would never again have sick animals in the place where we lived.

I considered myself a good deal better off in Inveranoch than in Glasgow because Loch Fyne was an arm of the sea that pushed up from the ocean down by Greenock right up into the Highlands as far as Cairndow and brought with it gulls to watch in flight and the smell of the sea and fish and queer birds to chase that ran along the beach behind which lay a wonderful dark and scary country of woods and glens and mountains of stone in which to hunt. I was never allowed out in Glasgow, but it was quite different here and soon I became a real Highlander and we Highlanders, of course, looked down on everyone else.

Inveranoch was not as large a city as Glasgow, in fact, it was quite small with no more than a few thousand inhabitants, but to make up for that hundreds of visitors came there every summer for their holidays.

This was the busiest time for Mr MacDhui for the guests often brought their pets with them, mostly dogs, of course, but sometimes also cats and birds, and once, a monkey, and the climate did not always agree with them or they would get themselves bitten or stung in the woods, or pick a fight with one of us Highlanders, which was foolish since they were much too soft and then their owners would have to bring them to Mr MacDhui for repairs. He seemed to take this in very ill part, for he was a man who hated pets and disliked being a veterinary and preferred to pass his time in the back country with the farmers and crofters rather than keep office hours.

However, none of this was any of my concern and I was fairly comfortable at this time, and living a routine sufficiently to my own taste, except for one thing. Mary Ruadh had become a cat carrier.

If you have had or have a little girl yourself you will know what I am talking about. If not, you may have noticed that at a certain age, little girls always carry a doll around wherever they go, but some carry their cats. Often they do not even know they are carrying it as they walk or toddle about with it. They hold it around the middle, just below the shoulders clutched to their breast so that most of the cat dangles a dead weight with head and forequarters hanging over the arm.

Mary Ruadh did vary this most uncomfortable and humiliating position sometimes by placing me across her shoulders like a fur piece

where I could rest and even be admired by people who sometimes said it was difficult to tell which was Mary Ruadh's hair and which was me. I didn't mind that. Or she would carry me upside down in both arms, like a little baby. I hated that.

If you ask me why I put up with it, I cannot tell you, since my philosophy of life is quite simple. When you find yourself in a situation where unpleasant things, or things you don't like, occur more frequently than pleasant ones – walk out.

Well, there were other things, too, which I wasn't going to mention, but as long as I am on the subject, I might as well. There was the being made to sit on a chair sometimes at tea with a napkin around my neck and pretend I was a person, or rather, Mary Ruadh pretended. This got me a few caraway seed cakes of which I happened to be fond and a couple of laps of milk out of a saucer, but it didn't make up for the indignity.

When I had kittens they took them away from me and drowned them.

At night I was forced to sleep at the foot of her bed. Nor could I go away to my favourite chair after she fell asleep for if she woke up and I was not there she would call for me and sob most heart-breakingly. Sometimes during the night, even when I was there, she would wake up and begin to cry softly in the darkness and murmur, 'Mummy – Mummy!' for it seems she remembered her, too. Then she would reach down in the darkness and wake me up and hold me to her so hard with her face buried in my flank that I could hardly breathe, and you know how we *hate* to be held.

She would then cry – 'Oh, Thomasina, Thomasina, I love you. Don't ever leave me.' After a little she would become more quiet and I would wash her face a little and lick the salt tears from her cheeks which made her laugh and giggle and say – 'Thomasina – you *tickle*,' and soon she would go to sleep again.

And I stayed on. Believe me, if it had been a little boy I should not have done so, thank you very much. I should soon enough have run away and not come back, taken to the woods or found someone else in town to live with, for I am perfectly capable of looking after Thomasina. Though I may look delicate, I am most resilient, have a hardy constitution and can stand almost anything. Once a boy on a bicycle ran over me. Mrs McKenzie came running out of the house screaming that I was killed and Mary Ruadh cried and carried on so that it took an hour afterwards to calm her and all that happened was that the boy fell off his bicycle and hurt himself and I got up and walked away.

Well, and then there was Mr MacDhui himself and there is plenty I could tell you about *him*, and none of it favourable. An animal doctor who didn't like animals, there's a good one. A bit too quick with the chloroform rag when people brought their sick pets to his surgery, was what they said. I'll tell you I wouldn't want him treating me. Mr MacDhui was jealous of me because his daughter loved me so much, and he hated me. But what was even worse, he *ignored* me. Mr High-and-mighty-around-the-house. Nose in the air, whiskers bristling all the time. And the medicine smell of him. Ugh! It was the same one that came out of the hospital when you went past. When he returned home at night and bent down to kiss Mary Ruadh his huge, bristly red face with the medicine and pipe smell would come right close to mine since Mary Ruadh would be carrying me, and it made me feel sick.

Naturally, I annoyed him all I could, calling attention to myself by washing in front of him, taking care to be on *his* chair when I knew he would be wanting it, lying in doorways where he would be likely to trip over me, rubbing up against his legs and ankles, leaving hairs on his best clothes whenever I could find them and jumping up on his lap

when he sat down to read the paper and making smells of my own. He did not dare to be rough with me when Mary Ruadh was in the room and so he would just pretend I was not there and then get up suddenly to go for some tobacco and dump me off his knees.

Add up all of these things and you might almost say it amounted to sufficient cause for me to move out. Yet I stayed on and was not too unhappy. I wouldn't have admitted it to anyone else, but if the truth be known, I was rather fond of the child.

I think it could have been because in some ways, girl children and cats are not un-alike. There is some special mystery about little girls, an attitude of knowing secret things and a contemplative and not wholly complimentary quality about the way they look at you sometimes that is often as baffling and exasperating to their elders, as we are.

If you have ever lived with a girl child, you will know that quiet, infuriating retirement into some private world of their own of which they are capable, as well as that stubborn independence in the face of stupid or unreasonable demands or prohibitions. These same traits seem to annoy you in us as well. For you can no more force a cat or a girl child to do something they do not wish to do than you can compel us to love you. We have this in common, Mary Ruadh and I.

Thus I did many strange things I should not have believed myself capable of doing. When Mary Ruadh went to school – this adventure of mine took place during the summer holidays – I suffered her to carry me all the way there, and to be pawed or fussed over by the other children until the bell rang and she went inside when I was free to run home and look after my business.

But, believe it or not, when it came time for her to come home in the afternoon I would be sitting up on the gate post with my tail curled round my legs, watching for her. True, it was also a fine vantage point from which to spit on the minister's pug dog when it went by, but nevertheless, there I was. The neighbours used to say you could always tell what time of day it was by the MacDhui cat getting up on to the gatepost to watch for her wee mistress.

I, Thomasina, waiting on a gatepost for a somewhat grubby, red-haired and not even especially beautiful child, can you imagine?

Sometimes I wondered whether there was not another bond between us: we were each to the other something to cling to when the sun goes down and nightfall brings on fear and loneliness.

Loneliness is comforted by the closeness and touch of fur to fur, skin to skin, or – skin to fur. Sometimes when I awoke at night after a bad dream, I would listen to the regular breathing of Mary Ruadh and

feel the slight rise and fall of the bedclothes about her. Then I would no longer be afraid and would go back to sleep again.

I have mentioned that Mary Ruadh was not an especially beautiful child, which perhaps was not polite, since she thought that I was certainly the most beautiful cat in the world, but I meant especially beautiful in the unusual sense. She was a rather ordinary looking little girl except for her eyes which told you of some special quality in her, or about her when you looked into them. Often I was not able to do so for long. Their colour was a bright blue, a most intense blue, but sometimes when she was thinking thoughts I could not understand or even guess, they turned as dark as the Loch on a stormy day.

For the rest, you wouldn't call her much to look at, with her uptilted nose and freckled face and a long lower lip that usually stuck out, while her eyebrows and lashes were so light you could hardly see them. She wore her ginger-red hair in two braids tied with green or blue ribbon. Her legs were quite long and she liked to stick her stomach out.

But there was something else pleasant about Mary Ruadh; she smelled good. Mrs McKenzie kept her washed and ironed when she was at home and she always smelled of lavender, for Mrs McKenzie kept lavender bags in with her clothes and underthings.

It seemed as if Mrs McKenzie was forever washing and ironing and starching and scenting her clothes, because it was the only way she was allowed to show how much she cared for Mary Ruadh. Mrs McKenzie was a thin woman who talked and sang through her nose. She would have mothered Mary Ruadh the way we will frequently look after somebody else's kitten as though it were our own, but Mr MacDhui was jealous and feared that Mary Ruadh would come to love her too much if she were allowed to cuddle her. Oh, Mr Bristle-and-Smelly was allowed to cuddle her all he wished, but nobody else.

I *loved* the odour of lavender. Smells, almost more than noises, seem to bring on the happiness or unhappiness memories. You might not remember what it was about a smell had made you angry at the time, or afraid, but as soon as you come across it again you are angry or fearful. Like the medicine smell of Mr MacDhui.

But lavender was the happiness smell. It made my claws move in and out and brought the contentment purr to my throat.

Sometimes after putting Mary Ruadh's things away after ironing them, Mrs McKenzie would forget to close all the chest of drawers, and leave one open. Then I would quickly nip inside and lie there full length with my nose up against a lavender bag, just smelling, smelling. That was bliss. That was when I was contented and at peace with the world.

Paul Gallico

(1897–1976)

Paul Gallico was an American author. For many years he wrote a popular sports column for a New York newspaper. He wrote his first novel, The Snow Goose *in 1941. Today, nearly fifty years later, it remains one of his best-known books. Paul Gallico was also the creator of Jean-Pierre the guinea-pig.*

CHARLOTTE'S WEB

Wilbur, the pig, runt of the litter, is saved from death by Fern Arable, the daughter of his owner. He is sent to live in her uncle, Mr Zuckerman's barn, and soon grows into a large and very fine pig indeed. Wilbur's life seems destined to be a happy one but he is lonely. Templeton the rat and in particular Charlotte A Cavatica the spider, not only give him friendship but also save Wilbur from the butcher's knife.

THE NEXT DAY WAS RAINY and dark. Rain fell on the roof of the barn and dripped steadily from the eaves. Rain fell in the barnyard and ran in crooked courses down into the lane where thistles and pigweed grew. Rain spattered against Mrs Zuckerman's kitchen windows and came gushing out of the downspouts. Rain fell on the backs of the sheep as they grazed in the meadow. When the sheep tired of standing in the rain, they walked slowly up the lane and into the fold.

Rain upset Wilbur's plans. Wilbur had planned to go out, this day, and dig a new hole in his yard. He had other plans, too. His plans for the day went something like this:

Breakfast at six-thirty. Skim milk, crusts, middlings, bits of doughnuts, wheat cakes with drops of maple syrup sticking to them, potato skins, left-over custard pudding with raisins, and bits of Shredded Wheat.

Breakfast would be finished at seven.

From seven to eight, Wilbur planned to have a talk with

Templeton, the rat that lived under his trough. Talking with Templeton was not the most interesting occupation in the world but it was better than nothing.

From eight to nine, Wilbur planned to take a nap outdoors in the sun.

From nine to eleven he planned to dig a hole, or trench, and possibly find something good to eat buried in the dirt.

From eleven to twelve he planned to stand still and watch flies on the boards, watch bees in the clover, and watch swallows in the air.

Twelve o'clock – lunchtime. Middlings, warm water, apple parings, meat gravy, carrot scrapings, meat scraps, stale hominy, and the wrapper off a package of cheese. Lunch would be over at one.

From one to two, Wilbur planned to sleep.

From two to three, he planned to scratch itchy places by rubbing against the fence.

From three to four, he planned to stand perfectly still and think of what it was like to be alive, and to wait for Fern.

At four would come supper. Skim milk, provender, left-over sandwich from Lurvy's lunchbox, prune skins, a morsel of this, a bit of that, fried potatoes, marmalade drippings, a little more of this, a little more of that, a piece of baked apple, a scrap of upside-down cake.

Wilbur had gone to sleep thinking about these plans. He awoke at six and saw the rain, and it seemed as though he couldn't bear it.

'I get everything all beautifully planned out and it has to go and rain,' he said.

For a while he stood gloomily indoors. Then he walked to the door and looked out. Drops of rain struck his face. His yard was cold and wet. His trough had an inch of rain water in it. Templeton was nowhere to be seen.

'Are you out there, Templeton?' called Wilbur. There was no answer. Suddenly Wilbur felt lonely and friendless.

'One day just like another,' he groaned. 'I'm very young, I have no real friend here in the barn, it's going to rain all morning and all afternoon, and Fern won't come in such bad weather. Oh, *honestly*!' And Wilbur was crying again, for the second time in two days.

At six-thirty Wilbur heard the banging of a pail. Lurvy was standing outside in the rain, stirring up breakfast.

'C'mon, pig!' said Lurvy.

Wilbur did not budge. Lurvy dumped the slops, scraped the pail, and walked away. He noticed that something was wrong with the pig.

Wilbur didn't want food, he wanted love. He wanted a friend –

someone who would play with him. He mentioned this to the goose, who was sitting quietly in a corner of the sheepfold.

'Will you come over and play with me?' he asked.

'Sorry, sonny, sorry,' said the goose. 'I'm sitting-sitting on my eggs. Eight of them. Got to keep them toasty-oasty-oasty warm. I have to stay right here, I'm no flibberty-ibberty-gibbet. I do not play when there are eggs to hatch. I'm expecting goslings.'

'Well, I didn't think you were expecting wood-peckers,' said Wilbur bitterly.

Wilbur next tried one of the lambs.

'Will you please play with me?' he asked.

'Certainly not,' said the lamb. 'In the first place, I cannot get into your pen, as I am not old enough to jump over the fence. In the second place, I am not interested in pigs. Pigs mean less than nothing to me.'

'What do you mean, *less* than nothing?' replied Wilbur. 'I don't think there is any such thing as *less* than nothing. Nothing is absolutely the limit of nothingness. It's the lowest you can go. It's the end of the line. How can something be less than nothing? If there were something that was less than nothing, then nothing would not be nothing, it would be something – even though it's just a very little bit of something. But if nothing is *nothing*, then nothing has nothing that is less than *it* is.'

'Oh, be quiet!' said the lamb. 'Go play by yourself! I don't play with pigs.'

Sadly, Wilbur lay down and listened to the rain. Soon he saw the rat climbing down a slanting board that he used as a stairway.

'Will you play with me, Templeton?' asked Wilbur.

'Play?' said Templeton, twirling his whiskers. 'Play? I hardly know the meaning of the word.'

'Well,' said Wilbur, 'it means to have fun, to frolic, to run and skip and make merry.'

'I never do those things if I can avoid them,' replied the rat, sourly. 'I prefer to spend my time eating, gnawing, spying, and hiding. I am a glutton but not a merrymaker. Right now I am on my way to your trough to eat your breakfast, since you haven't got sense enough to eat it yourself.' And Templeton, the rat, crept stealthily along the wall and disappeared into a private tunnel that he had dug between the door and the trough in Wilbur's yard. Templeton was a crafty rat, and he had things pretty much his own way. The tunnel was an example of his skill and cunning. The tunnel enabled him to get from the barn to his hiding-place under the pig trough without coming out into the open. He had tunnels and runways all over Mr Zuckerman's farm and could get from one place to another without being seen. Usually he slept during the daytime and was abroad only after dark.

Wilbur watched him disappear into his tunnel. In a moment he saw the rat's sharp nose poke out from underneath the wooden trough. Cautiously Templeton pulled himself up over the edge of the trough. This was almost more than Wilbur could stand: on this dreary, rainy day to see his breakfast being eaten by somebody else. He knew Templeton was getting soaked, out there in the pouring

rain, but even that didn't comfort him. Friendless, dejected, and hungry, he threw himself down in the manure and sobbed.

Late that afternoon, Lurvy went to Mr Zuckerman. 'I think there's something wrong with that pig of yours. He hasn't touched his food.'

'Give him two spoonfuls of sulphur and a little molasses,' said Mr Zuckerman.

Wilbur couldn't believe what was happening to him when Lurvy caught him and forced the medicine down his throat. This was certainly the worst day of his life. He didn't know whether he could endure the awful loneliness any more.

Darkness settled over everything. Soon there were only shadows and the noises of the sheep chewing their cuds, and occasionally the rattle of a cow-chain up overhead. You can imagine Wilbur's surprise when out of the darkness, came a small voice he had never heard before. It sounded rather thin, but pleasant. 'Do you want a friend, Wilbur?' it said. 'I'll be a friend to you. I've watched you all day and I like you.'

'But I can't see you,' said Wilbur, jumping to his feet. 'Where are you? And *who* are you?'

'I'm right up here,' said the voice. 'Go to sleep. You'll see me in the morning.'

The night seemed long. Wilbur's stomach was empty and his mind was full. And when your stomach is empty and your mind is full, it's always hard to sleep.

A dozen times during the night Wilbur woke and stared into the blackness, listening to the sounds and trying to figure out what time it was. A barn is never perfectly quiet. Even at midnight there is usually something stirring.

The first time he woke, he heard Templeton gnawing a hole in the grain bin. Templeton's teeth scraped loudly against the wood and made quite a racket. 'That crazy rat!' thought Wilbur. 'Why does he have to stay up all night, grinding his clashers and destroying people's property? Why can't he go to sleep, like any decent animal?'

The second time Wilbur woke, he heard the goose turning on her nest and chuckling to herself.

'What time is it?' whispered Wilbur to the goose.

'Probably-obably-obably about half-past eleven,' said the goose. 'Why aren't you asleep, Wilbur?'

'Too many things on my mind,' said Wilbur.

'Well,' said the goose, 'that's not *my* trouble. I have nothing at all on my mind, but I've too many things under my behind. Have you ever tried to sleep while sitting on eight eggs?'

'No,' replied Wilbur. 'I suppose it *is* uncomfortable. How long does it take a goose egg to hatch?'

'Approximately-oximately thirty days, all told,' answered the goose. 'But I cheat a little. On warm afternoons, I just pull a little straw over the eggs and go out for a walk.'

Wilbur yawned and went back to sleep. In his dreams he heard again the voice saying, 'I'll be a friend to you. Go to sleep – you'll see me in the morning.'

About half an hour before dawn, Wilbur woke and listened. The barn was still dark. The sheep lay motionless. Even the goose was quiet. Overhead, on the main floor, nothing stirred: the cows were resting, the horses dozed. Templeton had quit work and gone off somewhere on an errand. The only sound was a slight scraping noise from the rooftop, where the weather-vane swung back and forth. Wilbur loved the barn when it was like this – calm and quiet, waiting for light.

'Day is almost here,' he thought.

Through a small window, a faint gleam appeared. One by one the stars went out. Wilbur could see the goose a few feet away. She sat with head tucked under a wing. Then he could see the sheep and the lambs. The sky lightened.

'Oh, beautiful day, it is here at last! To-day I shall find my friend.'

Wilbur looked everywhere. He searched his pen thoroughly. He examined the window ledge, stared up at the ceiling. But he saw nothing new. Finally he decided he would have to speak up. He hated to break the lovely stillness of dawn by using his voice, but he couldn't think of any other way to locate the mysterious new friend who was nowhere to be seen. So Wilbur cleared his throat.

'Attention, please!' he said in a loud, firm voice. 'Will the party who addressed me at bedtime last night kindly make himself or herself known by giving an appropriate sign or signal!'

Wilbur paused and listened. All the other animals lifted their heads and stared at him. Wilbur blushed. But he was determined to get in touch with his unknown friend.

'Attention, please!' he said. 'I will repeat the message. Will the party who addressed me at bedtime last night kindly speak up. Please tell me where you are, if you are my friend!'

The sheep looked at each other in disgust.

'Stop your nonsense, Wilbur!' said the oldest sheep. 'If you have a new friend here, you are probably disturbing his rest; and the quickest way to spoil a friendship is to wake somebody up in the morning before he is ready. How can you be sure your friend in an early riser?'

'I beg everyone's pardon,' whispered Wilbur. 'I didn't mean to be objectionable.'

He lay down meekly in the manure, facing the door. He did not know it, but his friend was very near. And the old sheep was right – the friend was still asleep.

Soon Lurvy appeared with slops for breakfast. Wilbur rushed out, ate everything in a hurry, and licked the trough. The sheep moved off down the lane, the gander waddled along behind them, pulling grass. And then, just as Wilbur was settling down for his morning nap, he heard again the thin voice that had addressed him the night before.

'Salutations!' said the voice.

Wilbur jumped to his feet. 'Salu-*what*?' he cried.

'Salutations!' repeated the voice.

'What are *they*, and where are *you*?' screamed Wilbur. 'Please, *please*, tell me where you are. And what are salutations?'

'Salutations are greeting,' said the voice. 'When I say "salutations", it's just my fancy way of saying hello or good morning. Actually, it's a silly expression, and I am surprised that I used it at all. As for my whereabouts, that's easy. Look up here in the corner of the doorway! Here I am. Look, I'm waving!'

At last Wilbur saw the creature that had spoken to him in such a kindly way. Stretched across the upper part of the doorway was a big spider's web, and hanging from the top of the web, head down, was a large grey spider. She was about the size of a gum-drop. She had eight legs, and she was waving one of them at Wilbur in friendly greeting. 'See me now?' she asked.

'Oh, yes indeed,' said Wilbur. 'Yes indeed! How are you? Good morning! Salutations! Very pleased to meet you. What is your name, please? May I have your name?'

'My name,' said the spider, 'is Charlotte.'

'Charlotte what?' asked Wilbur, eagerly.

'Charlotte A. Cavatica. But just call me Charlotte.'

'I think you're beautiful,' said Wilbur.

'Well, I *am* pretty,' replied Charlotte. 'There's no denying that. Almost all spiders are rather nice-looking. I'm not as flashy as some, but I'll do. I wish I could see you, Wilbur, as clearly as you can see me.'

'Why can't you?' asked the pig. 'I'm right here.'

'Yes, but I'm near-sighted,' replied Charlotte. 'I've always been dreadfully near-sighted. It's good in some ways, not so good in others. Watch me wrap up this fly.'

A fly that had been crawling along Wilbur's trough had flown up and blundered into the lower part of Charlotte's web and was tangled in the sticky threads. The fly was beating its wings furiously, trying to break loose and free itself.

'First,' said Charlotte, 'I dive at him.' She plunged headfirst towards the fly. As she dropped, a tiny silken thread unwound from her rear end.

'Next, I wrap him up.' She grabbed the fly, threw a few jets of silk round it and rolled it over and over, wrapping it so that it couldn't move. Wilbur watched in horror. He could hardly beleve what he was seeing, and although he detested flies he was sorry for this one.

'There!' said Charlotte. 'Now I knock him out, so he'll be more comfortable.' She bit the fly. 'He can't feel a thing now,' she remarked. 'He'll make a perfect breakfast for me.'

'You mean you *eat* flies?' gasped Wilbur.

'Certainly. Flies, bugs, grasshoppers, choice beetles, moths, butterflies, tasty cockroaches, gnats, midges, daddy-long-legs, centipedes, mosquitoes, crickets – anything that is careless enough to get caught in my web. I have to live, don't I?'

'Why, yes, of course,' said Wilbur. 'Do they taste good?'

'Delicious. Of course, I don't really eat them. I drink them – drink their blood. I love blood,' said Charlotte, and her pleasant thin voice grew even thinner and more pleasant.

'Don't say that!' groaned Wilbur. 'Please don't say things like that!'

'Why not? It's true, and I have to say what is true. I am not entirely happy about my diet of flies and bugs, but it's the way I'm made. A spider has to pick up a living somehow or other, and I happen to be a trapper. I just naturally build a web and trap flies and other insects. My mother was a trapper before me. Her mother was a trapper before her. All our family have been trappers. Way back for thousands and thousands of years we spiders have been laying for flies and bugs.'

'It's a miserable inheritance,' said Wilbur, gloomily. He was sad because his new friend was so bloodthirsty.

'Yes, it is,' agreed Charlotte. 'But I can't help it. I don't know how the first spider in the early days of the world happened to think up this fancy idea of spinning a web, but she did, and it was clever of her, too. And since then, all of us spiders have had to work the same trick. It's not a bad pitch, on the whole.'

'It's cruel,' replied Wilbur, who did not intend to be argued out of his position.

'Well, *you* can't talk,' said Charlotte. '*You* have your meals brought to you in a pail. Nobody feeds me. I have to get my own living. I live by my wits. I have to be sharp and clever, lest I go hungry. I have to think things out, catch what I can, take what comes. And it just so happens, my friend, that what comes is flies and insects and bugs. And *furthermore*,' said Charlotte, shaking one of her legs, 'do you realize that if I didn't catch bugs and eat them, bugs would increase and multiply and get so numerous that they'd destroy the earth, wipe out everything?'

'Really?' said Wilbur. 'I wouldn't want *that* to happen. Perhaps your web is a good thing after all.'

The goose had been listening to this conversation and chuckling to herself. 'There are a lot of things Wilbur doesn't know about life,' she thought. 'He's really a very innocent little pig. He doesn't even know what's going to happen to him around Christmastime; he has no idea that Mr Zuckerman and Lurvy are plotting to kill him.' And the goose raised herself a bit and poked her eggs a little further under her so that they would receive the full heat from her warm body and soft feathers.

Charlotte stood quietly over the fly, preparing to eat it. Wilbur lay down and closed his eyes. He was tired from his wakeful night and from the excitement of meeting someone for the first time. A breeze brought him the smell of clover – the sweet-smelling world beyond his fence. 'Well,' he thought, 'I've got a new friend, all right. But what a gamble friendship is! Charlotte is fierce, brutal, scheming, bloodthirsty – everything I don't like. How can I learn to like her, even though she is pretty and, of course, clever?'

Wilbur was merely suffering the doubts and fears that often go with finding a new friend. In good time he was to discover that he was mistaken about Charlotte. Underneath her rather bold and cruel exterior, she had a kind heart, and she was to prove loyal and true to the very end.

E.B. White

(1899–1985)

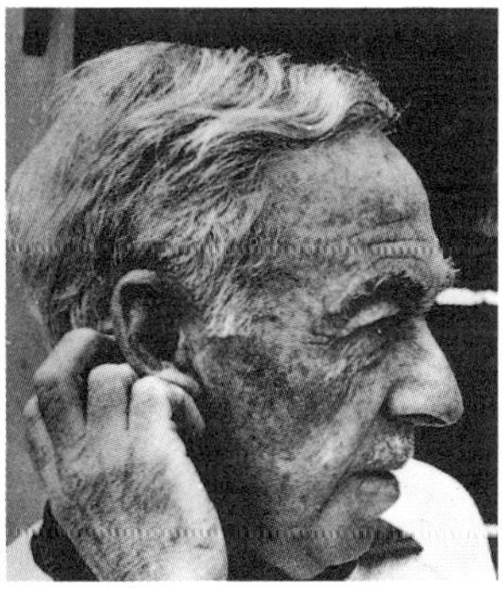

Elwyn Brooks White, the American writer, was born in 1899 and became famous for the humour of his books. His writing has been called "outstandingly funny". White's first book was published when he was 30 years old and since then, he has written for many well-known magazines in the United States. He won many awards and honours for his work.

THE HORSE AND HIS BOY

Narnia is a mythical land watched over by a godlike lion, Aslan. In this, the third of the Narnia chronicles, the best known of which is The Lion, the Witch and the Wardrobe, *the action of the story takes place on a journey into Narnia at a time when Peter, Edmund, Susan and Lucy (the central characters of* The Lion, the Witch and the Wardrobe*) ruled there, placed there by Aslan. This magical story begins in a poor fishing village in Calormen, a land bordering Narnia.*

THIS IS THE STORY of an adventure that happened in Narnia and Calormen and the lands between, in the Golden Age when Peter was High King in Narnia and his brother and his two sisters were King and Queens under him.

In those days, far south in Calormen on a little creek of the sea, there lived a poor fisherman called Arsheesh, and with him there lived a boy who called him Father. The boy's name was Shasta. On most days Arsheesh went out in his boat to fish in the morning, and in the afternoon he harnessed his donkey to a cart and loaded the cart with fish and went a mile or so southward to the village to sell it. If it had sold well he would come home in a moderately good temper and say nothing to Shasta, but if it had sold badly he would find fault with him and perhaps beat him. There was always something to find fault with for Shasta had plenty of work to do, mending and washing the nets, cooking the supper, and cleaning the cottage in which they both lived.

Shasta was not at all interested in anything that lay south of his home because he had once or twice been to the village with Arsheesh and he knew that there was nothing very interesting there. In the village he only met other men who were just like his father – men with long, dirty robes, and wooden shoes turned up at the toe, and turbans on their heads, and beards, talking to one another very slowly about things that sounded dull. But he was very interested in everything that lay to the North because no one ever went that way and he was never allowed to go there himself. When he was sitting out of doors mending the nets, and all alone, he would often look eagerly to the North. One could see nothing but a grassy slope running up to a level ridge and beyond that the sky with perhaps a few birds in it.

Sometimes if Arsheesh was there Shasta would say, 'O my Father, what is there beyond that hill?' And then if the fisherman was in a bad temper he would box Shasta's ears and tell him to attend to his work. Or if he was in a peaceable mood he would say, 'O my son, do not allow your mind to be distracted by idle questions. For one of the poets has said, "Application to business is the root of prosperity, but those who ask questions that do not concern them are steering the ship of folly towards the rock of indigence."'

Shasta thought that beyond the hill there must be some delightful secret which his father wished to hide from him. In reality, however, the fisherman talked like this because he didn't know what lay to the North. Neither did he care. He had a very practical mind.

One day there came from the south a stranger who was unlike any man that Shasta had seen before. He rode upon a strong dappled horse with flowing mane and tail and his stirrups and bridle were inlaid with silver. The spike of a helmet projected from the middle of his silken turban and he wore a shirt of chain mail. By his side hung a curving scimitar, a round shield studded with bosses of brass hung at his back, and his right hand grasped a lance. His face was dark, but this did not surprise Shasta because all the people of Calormen are like that; what did surprise him was the man's beard which was dyed crimson, and curled and gleaming with scented oil. But Arsheesh knew by the gold ring on the stranger's bare arm that he was a Tarkaan or great lord, and he bowed kneeling before him till his beard touched the earth and made signs to Shasta to kneel also.

The stranger demanded hospitality for the night which of course the fisherman dared not refuse. All the best they had was set before the Tarkaan for supper (and he didn't think much of it) and Shasta, as always happened when the fisherman had company, was given a hunk of bread and turned out of the cottage. On these occasions he usually slept with the donkey in its little thatched stable. But it was much too early to go to sleep yet, and Shasta, who had never learned that it is wrong to listen behind doors, sat down with his ear to a crack in the wooden wall of the cottage to hear what the grown-ups were talking about. And this is what he heard.

'And now, O my host,' said the Tarkaan, 'I have a mind to buy that boy of yours.'

'O my master,' replied the fisherman (and Shasta knew by the wheedling tone the greedy look that was probably coming into his face as he said it), 'what price could induce your servant, poor though he is, to sell into slavery his only child and his own flesh? Has not one of the poets said, "Natural affection is stronger than soup and offspring more precious than carbuncles?"'

'It is even so,' replied the guest dryly. 'But another poet has likewise said, "He who attempts to deceive the judicious is already baring his own back for the scourge." Do not load your aged mouth with falsehoods. This boy is manifestly no son of yours, for your cheek is as dark as mine but the boy is fair and white like the accursed but beautiful barbarians who inhabit the remote North.'

'How well it was said,' answered the fisherman, 'that Swords can be kept off with shields but the Eye of Wisdom pierces through every defence! Know then, O my formidable guest, that because of my extreme poverty I have never married and have no child. But in that same year in which the Tisroc (may he live for ever) began his august and beneficent reign, on a night when the moon was at her full, it pleased the gods to deprive me of my sleep. Therefore I arose from my bed in this hovel and went forth to the beach to refresh myself with looking upon the water and the moon and breathing the cool air. And presently I heard a noise as of oars coming to me across the water and then, as it were, a weak cry. And shortly after, the tide brought to the land a little boat in which there was nothing but a man lean with extreme hunger and thirst who seemed to have died but a few moments before (for he was still warm), and an empty water-skin, and a child, still living. "Doubtless," said I, "these unfortunates have escaped from the wreck of a great ship, but by the admirable designs of the gods, the elder has starved himself to keep the child alive and has perished in sight of land." Accordingly, remembering how the gods never fail to reward those who befriend the destitute, and being moved by compassion (for your servant is a man of tender heart)–'

'Leave out all these idle words in your own praise,' interrupted the Tarkaan. 'It is enough to know that you took the child – and have

had ten times the worth of his daily bread out of him in labour, as anyone can see. And now tell me at once what price you put on him, for I am wearied with you loquacity.'

'You yourself have wisely said,' answered Arsheesh, 'that the boy's labour has been to me of inestimable value. This must be taken into account in fixing the price. For if I sell the boy I must undoubtedly either buy or hire another to do his work.'

'I'll give you fifteen crescents for him,' said the Tarkaan.

'Fifteen!' cried Arsheesh in a voice that was something between a whine and a scream. 'Fifteen! For the prop of my old age and the delight of my eyes! Do not mock my grey beard, Tarkaan though you be. My price is seventy.'

At this point Shasta got up and tiptoed away. He had heard all he wanted, for he had often listened when men were bargaining in the village and knew how it was done. He was quite certain that Arsheesh would sell him in the end for something much more than fifteen crescents and much less than seventy, but that he and the Tarkaan would take hours in getting to an agreement.

You must not imagine that Shasta felt at all as you and I would feel if we had just overheard our parents talking about selling us for slaves. For one thing, his life was already little better than slavery; for all he knew, the lordly stranger on the great horse might be kinder to him than Arsheesh. For another, the story about his own discovery in the boat had filled him with excitement and with a sense of relief. He had often been uneasy because, try as he might, he had never been able to love the fisherman, and he knew that a boy ought to love his father. And now, apparently, he was no relation to Arsheesh at all. That took a great weight off his mind. 'Why I might be anyone!' he thought. 'I might be the son of a Tarkaan myself – or the son of the Tisroc (may he live for ever) – or of a god!'

He was standing out in the grassy place before the cottage while he thought these things. Twilight was coming on apace and a star or two was already out, but the remains of the sunset could still be seen in the west. Not far away the stranger's horse, loosely tied to an iron ring in the wall of the donkey's stable, was grazing. Shasta strolled over to it and patted its neck. It went on tearing up the grass and took no notice of him.

Then another thought came into Shasta's mind. 'I wonder what sort of a man that Tarkaan is,' he said out loud. 'It would be splendid if he was kind. Some of the slaves in a great lord's house have next to nothing to do. They wear lovely clothes and eat meat every day. Perhaps he'd take me to the wars and I'd save his life in a battle and then he'd set me free and adopt me as his son and give me a palace and a chariot and a suit of armour. But then he might be a horrid, cruel man. He might send me to work on the fields in chains. I wish I knew. How can I know? I bet this horse knows, if only he could tell me.'

The Horse had lifted its head. Shasta stroked its smooth-as-satin nose and said, 'I wish *you* could talk, old fellow.'

And then for a second he thought he was dreaming, for quite distinctly, though in a low voice, the Horse said, 'But I can.'

Shasta stared into its great eyes and his own grew almost as big, with astonishment.

'How ever did *you* learn to talk?' he asked.

'Hush! Not so loud,' replied the Horse. 'Where I come from, nearly all the animals talk.'

'Wherever is that?' asked Shasta.

'Narnia,' answered the Horse. 'The happy land of Narnia – Narnia of the heathery mountains and the thymy downs, Narnia of the many rivers, the plashing glens, the mossy caverns and the deep forests

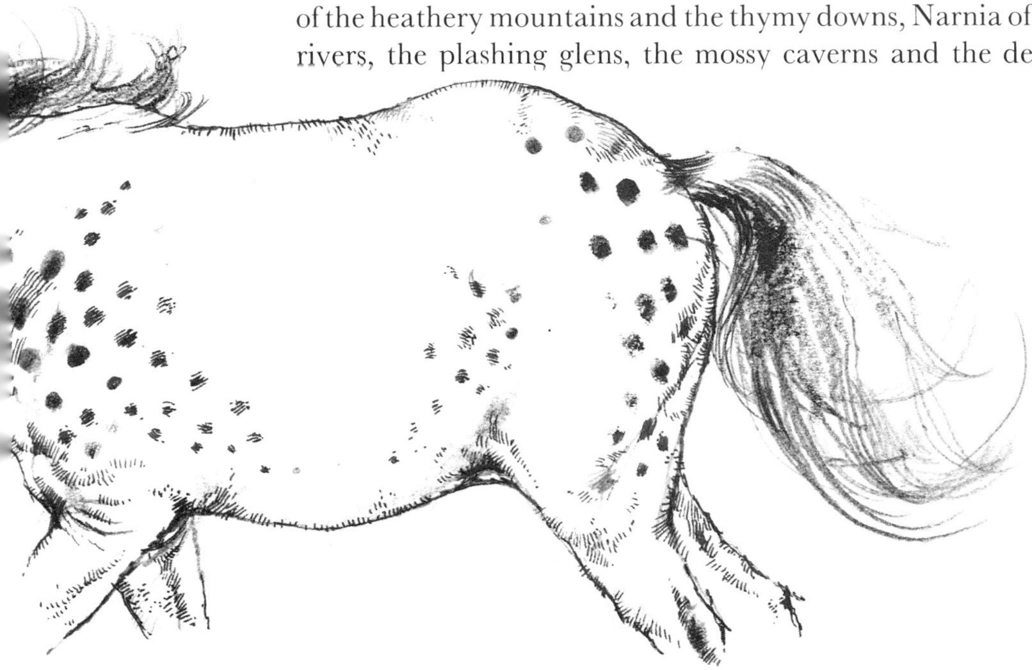

ringing with the hammers of the Dwarfs. Oh the sweet air of Narnia! An hour's life there is better than a thousand years in Calormen.' It ended with a whinny that sounded very like a sigh.

'How did you get here?' said Shasta.

'Kidnapped,' said the Horse. 'Or stolen, or captured – whichever you like to call it. I was only a foal at the time. My mother warned me not to range the southern slopes, into Archenland and beyond, but I wouldn't heed her. And by the Lion's Mane I have paid for my folly. All these years I have been a slave to humans, hiding my true nature and pretending to be dumb and witless like *their* horses.'

'Why didn't you tell them who you were?'

'Not such a fool, that's why. If they'd once found out I could talk they would have made a show of me at fairs and guarded me more carefully than ever. My last chance of escape would have been gone.'

'And why –' began Shasta, but the Horse interrupted him.

'Now look,' it said, 'we mustn't waste time on idle questions. You want to know about my master the Tarkaan Anradin. Well, he's bad. Not too bad to me, for a war horse costs too much to be treated very badly. But you'd be better lying dead tonight than go to be a human slave in his house tomorrow.'

'Then I'd better run away,' said Shasta, turning very pale.

'Yes, you had,' said the Horse. 'But why not run away with me?'

'Are you going to run away too?' said Shasta.

'Yes, if you'll come with me,' answered the Horse. 'This is the chance for both of us. You see if I run away without a rider, everyone who sees me will say "Stray horse" and be after me as quick as he can. With a rider I've a chance to get through. That's where you can help me. On the other hand, you can't get very far on those two silly legs of yours (what absurd legs humans have!) without being overtaken. But on me you can outdistance any other horse in this country. That's where I can help you. By the way, I suppose you know how to ride?'

'Oh yes, of course,' said Shasta. 'At least, I've ridden the donkey.'

'Ridden the *what*?' retorted the Horse with extreme contempt. (At least, that is what he meant. Actually it came out in a sort of neigh – 'Ridden the wha-ha-ha-ha-ha.' Talking horses always become more horsy in accent when they are angry.)

'In other words,' it continued, 'you *can't* ride. That's a drawback. I'll have to teach you as we go along. If you can't ride, can you fall?'

'I suppose anyone can fall,' said Shasta.

'I mean can you fall and get up again without crying and mount again and fall again and yet not be afraid of falling?'

'I-I'll try,' said Shasta.

'Poor little beast,' said the Horse in a gentler tone. 'I forget you're only a foal. We'll make a fine rider of you in time. And now – we mustn't start until those two in the hut are asleep. Meantime we can make our plans. My Tarkaan is on his way North to the great city, to Tashbaan itself and the court of the Tisroc –'

'I say,' put in Shasta in rather a shocked voice, 'oughtn't you to say "May he live for ever?"'

'Why?' asked the Horse. 'I'm a free Narnian. And why should I talk slaves' and fools' talk? I don't want him to live for ever, and I know that he's not going to live for ever whether I want him to or not. And I can see you're from the free North too. No more of this Southern jargon between you and me! And now, back to our plans. As I said, my human was on his way North to Tashbaan.'

'Does that mean we'd better go to the South?'

'I think not,' said the Horse. 'You see, he thinks I'm dumb and witless like his other horses. Now if I really were, the moment I got loose I'd go back home to my stable and paddock; back to his palace which is two days' journey South. That's where he'll look for me. He'd never dream of my going on North on my own. And anyway he will probably think that someone in the last village who saw him ride through has followed us to here and stolen me.'

'Oh hurrah!' said Shasta. 'Then we'll go North. I've been longing to go to the North all my life.'

'Of course you have,' said the Horse. 'That's because of the blood that's in you. I'm sure you're true Northern stock. But not too loud. I should think they'd be asleep soon now.'

'I'd better creep back and see,' suggested Shasta.

'That's a good idea,' said the Horse. 'But take care you're not caught.'

It was a good deal darker now and very silent except for the sound of the waves on the beach, which Shasta hardly noticed because he had been hearing it day and night as long as he could remember. The cottage, as he approached it, showed no light. When he listened at the front there was no noise. When he went round to the only window, he could hear, after a second or two, the familiar noise of the old fisherman's squeaky snore. It was funny to think that if all went well he would never hear it again. Holding his breath and feeling a little bit sorry, but much less sorry than he was glad, Shasta glided away

over the grass and went to the donkey's stable, groped along to a place he knew where the key was hidden, opened the door and found the Horse's saddle and bridle which had been locked up there for the night. He bent forward and kissed the donkey's nose. 'I'm sorry we can't take *you*,' he said.

'There you are at last,' said the Horse when he got back to it. 'I was beginning to wonder what had become of you.'

'I was getting your things out of the stable,' replied Shasta. 'And now, can you tell me how to put them on?'

For the next few minutes Shasta was at work, very cautiously to avoid jingling, while the Horse said things like, 'Get that girth a bit tighter,' or 'You'll find a buckle lower down,' or 'You'll need to shorten those stirrups a good bit.' When all was finished it said:

'Now; we've got to have reins for the look of the thing, but you won't be using them. Tie them to the saddle-bow: very slack so that I can do what I like with my head. And, remember – you are not to touch them.'

'What are they for, then?' asked Shasta.

'Ordinarily they are for directing me,' replied the Horse. 'But as I intend to do all the directing on this journey, you'll please keep your hands to yourself. And there's another thing. I'm not going to have you grabbing my mane.'

'But I say,' pleaded Shasta. 'If I'm not to hold on by the reins or by your mane, what *am* I to hold on by?'

'You hold on with your knees,' said the Horse. 'That's the secret of good riding. Grip my body between your knees as hard as you like; sit straight up, straight as a poker; keep your elbows in. And by the way, what did you do with the spurs?'

'Put them on my heels, of course,' said Shasta. 'I do know that much.'

'Then you can take them off and put them in the saddle-bag. We may be able to sell them when we get to Tashbaan. Ready? And now I think you can get up.'

'Ooh! You're a dreadful height,' gasped Shasta after his first, and unsuccessful, attempt.

'I'm a horse, that's all,' was the reply. 'Anyone would think I was a haystack from the way you're trying to climb up me! There, that's better. Now sit *up* and remember what I told you about your knees. Funny to think of me who has led cavalry charges and won races having a potato-sack like you in the saddle! However, off we go.' It chuckled, not unkindly.

And it certainly began their night journey with great caution. First of all it went just south of the fisherman's cottage to the little river which there ran into the sea, and took care to leave in the mud some very plain hoof-marks pointing South. But as soon as they were in the middle of the ford it turned upstream and waded till they were about a hundred yards farther inland than the cottage. Then it selected a nice gravelly bit of bank which would take no footprints and came out on the Northern side. Then, still at a walking pace, it went Northward till the cottage, the one tree, the donkey's stable, and the creek – everything, in fact, that Shasta had ever known – had sunk out of sight in the grey summer-night darkness. They had been going uphill and now were at the top of the ridge – that ridge which had always been the boundary of Shasta's known world. He could not see what was ahead except that it was all open and grassy. It looked endless: wild and lonely and free.

'I say!' observed the Horse. 'What a place for a gallop, eh?'

'Oh don't let's,' said Shasta. 'Not yet. I don't know how to – please, Horse. I don't know your name.'

'Breehy-hinny-brinny-hoohy-hah,' said the Horse.

'I'll never be able to say that,' said Shasta. 'Can I call you Bree?'

'Well, if it's the best you can do, I suppose you must,' said the Horse. 'And what shall I call you?'

'I'm called Shasta.'

'H'm,' said Bree. 'Well, now, there's a name that's *really* hard to pronounce. But now about this gallop. It's a good deal easier than trotting if you only knew, because you don't have to rise and fall. Grip

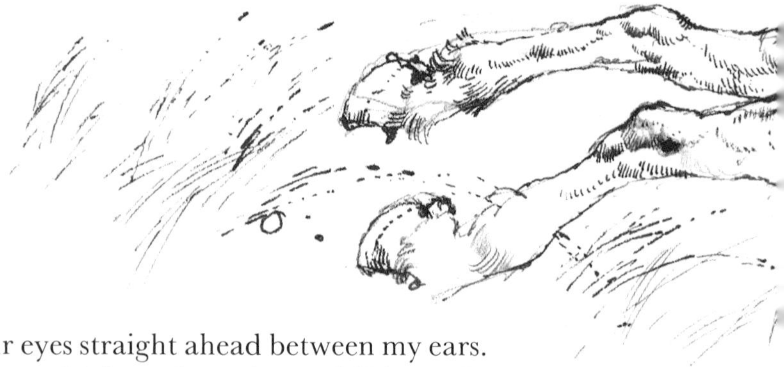

with your knees and keep your eyes straight ahead between my ears. Don't look at the ground. If you think you're going to fall just grip harder and sit up straighter. Ready? Now: for Narnia and the North.'

It was nearly noon on the following day when Shasta was wakened by something warm and soft moving over his face. He opened his eyes and found himself staring into the long face of a horse; its nose and lips were almost touching his. He remembered the exciting events of the previous night and sat up. But as he did so he groaned.

'Ow, Bree,' he gasped. 'I'm so sore. All over. I can hardly move.'

'Good morning, small one,' said Bree. 'I was afraid you might feel a bit stiff. It can't be the falls. You didn't have more than a dozen or so and it was all lovely, soft springy turf that must have been almost a pleasure to fall on. And the only one that might have been nasty was broken by that gorse bush. No: it's the riding itself that comes hard at first. What about breakfast? I've had mine.'

'Oh bother breakfast. Bother everything,' said Shasta. 'I tell you I can't move.' But the horse nuzzled at him with its nose and pawed him gently with a hoof till he had to get up. And then he looked about him and saw where they were. Behind them lay a little copse. Before them the turf, dotted with white flowers, sloped down to the brow of a cliff. Far below them, so that the sound of the breaking waves was very faint, lay the sea. Shasta had never seen it from such a height and never seen so much of it before, nor dreamed how many colours it had. On either hand the coast stretched away, headland after headland, and at the points you could see the white foam running up the rocks but making no noise because it was so far off. There were gulls flying overhead and the heat shivered on the ground; it was a

blazing day. But what Shasta chiefly noticed was the air. He couldn't think what was missing, until at last he realized that there was no smell of fish in it. For of course, neither in the cottage nor among the nets, had he ever been away from that smell in his life. And this new air was so delicious, and all his old life seemed so far away, that he forgot for a moment about his bruises and his aching muscles and said:

'I say, Bree, didn't you say something about breakfast?'

'Yes, I did,' answered Bree. 'I think you'll find something in the saddle-bags. They're over there on that tree where you hung them up last night – or early this morning, rather.'

They investigated the saddle-bags and the results were cheering – a meat pasty, only slightly stale, a lump of dried figs and another lump of green cheese, a little flask of wine, and some money; about forty crescents in all, which was more than Shasta had ever seen.

While Shasta sat down – painfully and cautiously – with his back against a tree and started on the pasty, Bree had a few more mouthfuls of grass to keep him company.

'Won't it be stealing to use the money?' asked Shasta.

'Oh,' said the Horse, looking up with its mouth full of grass, 'I

never thought of that. A free horse and a talking horse mustn't steal, of course. But I think it's all right. We're prisoners and captives in enemy country. That money is booty, spoil. Besides, how are we to get any food for you without it? I suppose, like all humans, you won't eat natural food like grass and oats.'

'I can't.'

'Ever tried?'

'Yes, I have. I can't get it down at all. You couldn't either if you were me.'

'You're rum little creatures, you humans,' remarked Bree.

When Shasta had finished his breakfast (which was by far the nicest he had ever eaten), Bree said, 'I think I'll have a nice roll before we put on that saddle again.' And he proceeded to do so. 'That's good. That's very good,' he said, rubbing his back on the turf and waving all four legs in the air. 'You ought to have one too, Shasta,' he snorted. 'It's most refreshing.'

But Shasta burst out laughing and said, 'You do look funny when you're on your back!'

'I look nothing of the sort,' said Bree. But then suddenly he rolled round on his side, raised his head and looked hard at Shasta, blowing a little.

'Does it really look funny?' he asked in an anxious voice.

'Yes, it does,' replied Shasta. 'But what does it matter?'

'You don't think, do you,' said Bree, 'that it might be a thing *talking* horses never do – a silly, clownish trick I've learned from the dumb ones? It would be dreadful to find, when I get back to Narnia, that I've picked up a lot of low, bad habits. What do you think, Shasta? Honestly, now. Don't spare my feelings. Should you think the real, free horses – the talking kind – do roll?'

'How should I know? Anyway I don't think I should bother about it if I were you. We've got to get there first. Do you know the way?'

'I know my way to Tashbaan. After that comes the desert. Oh, we'll manage the desert somehow, never fear. Why, we'll be in sight of the Northern mountains then. Think of it! To Narnia and the North! Nothing will stop us then. But I'd be glad to be past Tashbaan. You and I are safer away from cities.'

'Can't we avoid it?'

'Not without going a long way inland, and that would take us into cultivated land and main roads; and I wouldn't know the way. No, we'll just have to creep along the coast. Up here on the downs we'll meet nothing but sheep and rabbits and gulls and a few shepherds. And by the way, what about starting?'

Shasta's legs ached terribly as he saddled Bree and climbed into the saddle, but the Horse was kindly to him and went at a soft pace all afternoon. When evening twilight came they dropped by steep tracks into a valley and found a village. Before they got into it Shasta dismounted and entered it on foot to buy a loaf and some onions and radishes. The Horse trotted round by the fields in the dusk and met Shasta at the far side. This became their regular plan every second night.

These were great days for Shasta, and every day better than the last as his muscles hardened and he fell less often. Even at the end of his training Bree still said he sat like a bag of flour in the saddle. 'And even if it was safe, young 'un, I'd be ashamed to be seen with you on the main road.' But in spite of his rude words Bree was a patient teacher. No one can teach riding so well as a horse. Shasta learned to trot, to canter, to jump, and to keep his seat even when Bree pulled up suddenly or swung unexpectedly to the left or the right – which, as Bree told him, was a thing you might have to do at any moment in a battle. And then of course Shasta begged to be told of the battles and wars in which Bree had carried the Tarkaan. And Bree would tell of forced marches and the fording of swift rivers, of charges and of fierce fights between cavalry and cavalry when the war horses fought as well as the men, being all fierce stallions, trained to bite and kick, and to rear at the right moment so that the horse's weight as well as the rider's would come down on an enemy's crest in the stroke of sword or battleaxe. But Bree did not want to talk about the wars as often as Shasta wanted to hear about them. 'Don't speak of them, youngster,' he would say. 'They were only the Tisroc's wars and I fought in them as a slave and a dumb beast. Give me the Narnian wars where I shall fight as a free Horse among my own people! Those will be wars worth talking about. Narnia and the North! Bra-ha-ha! Broo hoo!'

Shasta soon learned, when he heard Bree talking like that, to prepare for a gallop.

After they had travelled on for weeks and weeks past more bays and headlands and rivers and villages than Shasta could remember, there came a moonlit night when they started their journey at evening, having slept during the day. They had left the downs behind them and were crossing a wide plain with a forest about half a mile away on their left. The sea, hidden by low sandhills, was about the same distance on their right. They had jogged along for about an hour, sometimes trotting and sometimes walking, when Bree suddenly stopped.

'What's up?' said Shasta.

'S-s-ssh!' said Bree, craning his neck round and twitching his ears. 'Did you hear something? Listen.'

'It sounds like another horse – between us and the wood,' said Shasta after he had listened for about a minute.

'It *is* another horse,' said Bree. 'And that's what I don't like.'

'Isn't it probably just a farmer riding home late?' said Shasta with a yawn.

'Don't tell me!' said Bree. '*That's* not a farmer's riding. Nor a farmer's horse either. Can't you tell by the sound? That's quality, that horse is. And it's being ridden by a real horseman. I tell you what it is, Shasta. There's a Tarkaan under the edge of that wood. Not on his war horse – it's too light for that. On a fine blood mare, I should say.'

'Well, it's stopped now, whatever it is,' said Shasta.

'You're right,' said Bree. 'And why should he stop just when we do? Shasta, my boy, I do believe there's someone shadowing us at last.'

'What shall we do?' said Shasta in a lower whisper than before. 'Do you think he can see us as well as hear us?'

'Not in this light so long as we stay quite still,' answered Bree. 'But look! There's a cloud coming up. I'll wait till that gets over the moon. Then we'll get off to our right as quietly as we can, down to the shore. We can hide among the sandhills if the worst comes to the worst.'

They waited till the cloud covered the moon and then, first at a walking pace and afterwards at a gentle trot, made for the shore.

The cloud was bigger and thicker than it had looked at first and soon the night grew very dark. Just as Shasta was saying to himself, 'We must be nearly at those sandhills by now,' his heart leaped into his mouth because an appalling noise had suddenly risen up out of the darkness ahead; a long snarling roar, melancholy and utterly savage. Instantly Bree swerved round and began galloping inland again as fast as he could gallop.

'What is it?' gasped Shasta.

'Lions!' said Bree, without checking his pace or turning his head.

After that there was nothing but sheer galloping for some time. At last they splashed across a wide, shallow stream and Bree came to a stop on the far side. Shasta noticed that he was trembling and sweating all over.

'That water may have thrown the brute off our scent,' panted Bree when he had partly got his breath again. 'We can walk for a bit now.'

As they walked Bree said, 'Shasta, I'm ashamed of myself. I'm just as frightened as a common, dumb Calormene horse. I am really. I don't feel like a Talking Horse at all. I don't mind swords and lances and arrows but I can't bear – those creatures. I think I'll trot for a bit.'

About a minute later, however, he broke into a gallop again, and no wonder. For the roar broke out again, this time on their left from the direction of the forest.

'Two of them,' moaned Bree.

When they had galloped for several minute without any further noise from the lions Shasta said, 'I say! That other horse is galloping beside us now. Only a stone's throw away.'

'All the be-better,' panted Bree. 'Tarkaan on it – will have a sword – protect us all.'

'But, Bree!' said Shasta. 'We might just as well be killed by lions as caught. Or *I* might. They'll hang me for horse-stealing.' He was feeling less frightened of lions than Bree because he had never met a lion; Bree had.

Bree only snorted in answer but he did sheer away to his right. Oddly enough the other horse seemed also to be sheering away to the left, so that in a few seconds the space between them had widened a good deal. But as soon as it did so there came two more lions' roars, immediately after one another, one on the right and the other on the left, and the horses began drawing nearer together. So, apparently, did the lions. The roaring of the brutes on each side was horribly close and they seemed to be keeping up with the galloping horses quite easily. Then the cloud rolled away. The moonlight, astonishingly bright, showed up everything almost as if it were broad day. The two horses and the two riders were galloping neck to neck and knee to knee just as if they were in a race. Indeed Bree said (afterwards) that a finer race had never been seen in Calormen.

Shasta now gave himself up for lost and began to wonder whether lions killed you quickly or played with you as a cat plays with a mouse and how much it would hurt. At the same time (one sometimes does this at the most frightful moments) he noticed everything. He saw that the other rider was a very small, slender person, mail-clad (the moon shone on the mail) and riding magnificently. He had no beard.

Something flat and shining was spread out before them. Before Shasta had time even to guess what it was there was a great splash and he found his mouth half full of salt water. The shining thing had been a long inlet of the sea. Both horses were swimming and the water was up to Shasta's knees. There was an angry roaring behind them and looking back Shasta saw a great, shaggy, and terrible shape crouched on the water's edge; but only one. 'We must have shaken off the other lion,' he thought.

The lion apparently did not think its prey worth a wetting; at any rate it made no attempt to take the water in pursuit. The two horses, side by side, were now well out into the middle of the creek and the opposite shore could be clearly seen. The Tarkaan had not yet spoken a word. 'But he will,' thought Shasta. 'As soon as we have landed. What am I to say? I must begin thinking out a story.'

Then, suddenly, two voices spoke at his side.

'Oh, I *am* so tired,' said the one.

'Hold your tongue, Hwin, and don't be a fool,' said the other.

'I'm dreaming,' thought Shasta. 'I could have sworn that other horse spoke.'

Soon the horses were no longer swimming but walking and soon with a great sound of water running off their sides and tails and with a great crunching of pebbles under eight hoofs, they came out on the farther beach of the inlet. The Tarkaan, to Shasta's surprise, showed no wish to ask questions. He did not even look at Shasta but seemed anxious to urge his horse straight on. Bree, however, at once shouldered himself in the other horse's way.

'Broo-hoo-hah!' he snorted. 'Steady there! I *heard* you, I did. There's no good pretending, Ma'am. I heard you. You're a Talking Horse, a Narnian horse just like me.'

'What's it got to do with you if she is?' said the strange rider fiercely, laying hand on sword-hilt. But the voice in which the words were spoken had already told Shasta something.

'Why, it's only a girl!' he exclaimed.

'And what business is it of yours if I am *only* a girl?' snapped the stranger. 'You're only a boy: a rude, common little boy – a slave probably, who's stolen his master's horse.'

'That's all *you* know,' said Shasta.

'He's not a thief, little Tarkheena,' said Bree. 'At least, if there's been any stealing, you might just as well say I stole *him*. And as for its not being my business, you wouldn't expect me to pass a lady of my own race in this strange country without speaking to her? It's only natural I should.'

'I think it's very natural too,' said the mare.

'I wish you'd held your tongue, Hwin,' said the girl. 'Look at the trouble you've got us into.'

'I don't know about trouble,' said Shasta. 'You can clear off as soon as you like. We shan't keep you.'

'No, you shan't,' said the girl.

'What quarrelsome creatures these humans are,' said Bree to the mare. 'They're as bad as mules. Let's try to talk a little sense. I take it, Ma'am, your story is the same as mine? Captured in early youth – years of slavery among the Calormenes?'

'Too true, sir,' said the mare with a melancholy whinny.

'And now, perhaps – escape?'

'Tell him to mind his own business, Hwin,' said the girl.

'No, I won't, Aravis,' said the mare, putting her ears back. 'This is my escape just as much as yours. And I'm sure a noble war-horse like this is not going to betray us. We are trying to escape, to get to Narnia.'

'And so, of course, are we,' said Bree. 'Of course you guessed that at once. A little boy in rags riding (or trying to ride) a war-horse at dead of night couldn't mean anything but an escape of some sort. And, if I may say so, a high-born Tarkheena riding alone at night – dressed up in her brother's armour – and very anxious for everyone to mind their own business and ask her no questions – well, if that's not fishy, call me a cob!'

'All right then,' said Aravis. 'You've guessed it. Hwin and I are running away. We are trying to get to Narnia. And now, what about it?'

'Why, in that case, what is to prevent us all going together?' said Bree. 'I trust, Madam Hwin, you will accept such assistance and protection as I may be able to give you on the journey?'

'Why do you keep on talking to my horse instead of to me?' asked the girl.

'Excuse me, Tarkheena,' said Bree (with just the slightest backward tilt of his ears), 'but that's Calormene talk. We're free Narnians, Hwin and I, and I suppose, if you're running away to Narnia, you want to be one too. In that case Hwin isn't *your* horse any longer. One might just as well say you're *her* human.'

The girl opened her mouth to speak and then stopped. Obviously she had not quite seen it in that light before.

'Still,' she said after a moment's pause, 'I don't know that there's so much point in all going together. Aren't we more likely to be noticed?'

'Less,' said Bree; and the mare said, 'Oh do let's. I should feel much more comfortable. We're not even certain of the way. I'm sure a great charger like this knows far more than we do.'

'Oh come on, Bree,' said Shasta, 'and let them go their own way. Can't you see they don't want us?'

'We do,' said Hwin.

'Look here,' said the girl. 'I don't mind going with *you*, Mr War-Horse, but what about this boy? How do I know he's not a spy?'

'Why don't you say at once that you think I'm not good enough for you?' said Shasta.

'Be quiet, Shasta,' said Bree. 'The Tarkheena's question is quite reasonable. I'll vouch for the boy, Tarkheena. He's been true to me and a good friend. And he's certainly either a Narnian or an Archenlander.'

'All right, then. Let's go together.' But she didn't say anything to Shasta and it was obvious that she wanted Bree, not him.

'Splendid!' said Bree. 'And now that we've got the water between us and those dreadful animals, what about you two humans taking off our saddles and our all having a rest and hearing one another's stories.'

Both the children unsaddled their horses and the horses had a little grass and Aravis produced rather nice things to eat from her saddle-bag. But Shasta sulked and said No thanks, and that he wasn't hungry. And he tried to put on what he thought very grand and stiff manners, but as a fisherman's hut is not usually a good place for learning grand manners, the result was dreadful. And he half knew that it wasn't a success and then became sulkier and more awkward than ever. Meanwhile the two horses were getting on splendidly. They remembered the very same places in Narnia – 'the grasslands up above Beaversdam' and found that they were some sort of second cousins once removed. This made things more and more uncomfortable for the humans until at last Bree said, 'And now, Tarkheena, tell us your story. And don't hurry it – I'm feeling comfortable now.'

Aravis immediately began, sitting quite still and using a rather different tone and style from her usual one. For in Calormen, story-telling (whether the stories are true or made up) is a thing you're taught, just as English boys and girls are taught essay-writing. The difference is that people want to hear the stories, whereas I never heard of anyone who wanted to read the essays.

C.S. Lewis

(1898–1963)

Clive Staples Lewis, the son of a solicitor, was born in Belfast. A brilliant scholar, he became a Professor of Literature and taught first at Oxford and later at Cambridge University. Though he became an atheist as a young man, his faith in Christianity was restored in 1931. Afterwards, Lewis expressed his regained religion in his own writings. He began writing children's books after the War. In these books, his aim was to make Christianity easily understandable to ordinary people of all ages.

THE MOUSE BUTCHER

Tom Plug, once a butcher's cat, is renowned for his bravery and ability as a hunter. In the middle of the deserted island on which Tom lives is Hobb's Hole, a leafy pit, in which legend has it, lives a wild monster. Only Tom is bold enough to confront the unknown monster of Hobb's Hole.

THE FITTEST ANIMALS, as everyone knows, stand the best chance of survival. And the mouse that poked his face out of the tumble-down shed at the back of the deserted butcher's shop was very fit indeed. He could run faster and squeak louder and eat quicker than the rest of his tribe, and his eyes and his ears were as sharp as his nose.

Alas, he was proud of his powers, and pride, as everyone knows, comes before a fall. If only he had run straight from the shed into one of the grass-tunnels in the matted ruin of a lawn, if only he hadn't stopped to arrange his whiskers, if only a precious second had not gone by while he said to himself, 'I am the greatest.'

But the pause and the preening and the pride made that precious second his last. Black death dropped from the top of the broken garden wall and white teeth cut off his final squeak.

Tom Plug was very black. He wasn't particularly big but he was sleek and muscular. Short-haired, green-eyed, sharp-clawed, he looked what he was – a hunter. Unlike most cats, he did not play with his victim. That first bite killed it, and now he split and gutted it with professional skill. His strong jaws made short work of the meal, and soon the tail and back legs were all that was left of the greatest mouse.

Later that morning, Tom lay upon the bare marble slab in the window of the empty shop and gazed down the deserted village street. There were gaping holes in some roofs where tiles had been blown off, paintwork everywhere was drab and peeling, and gardens were wildly overgrown and choked with weeds and tall grasses. Outside, above the shop-front, the faded lettering still read, *Percy J. Plug. Pork Butcher*, but it was more than twelve moons now since Tom had last seen the man; the remains of his blue-striped apron and his straw hat still hung behind the door, but the mice had dealt hardly with them. The once scrubbed and scoured surfaces of the heavy wooden tables bore nothing but mouse-dirt and snail-trails, the brown stains on the rows of knives and cleavers and saws were not of blood but of rust, and from the big steel hooks in the ceiling hung only spiders' webs.

Opposite Tom lay his elderly friend Giglamps Macdonald, once the doctor's cat. He had long ginger fur, a white bib and paws, and, curiously, white rings like spectacles around his yellow eyes.

In the old days doctor and butcher had only met when one needed meat or the other medicine, and their cats had not met at all. But one morning not long after the humans had gone, Tom Plug, swinging along the village street with a mouse in his mouth, had noticed a ginger-and-white cat sitting outside a front door with a discoloured brass plate set in it. *Dr I. Macdonald MD MRCP*, it said. Tom could not read this, but he could read the hungry look on the ginger cat's face and on an impulse he dropped the mouse on the pavement in front of him. So their friendship had been born.

Tom stuck out a foreleg to its fullest extent. He spread his toes, unsheathed his claws, and regarded them thoughtfully.

'Mmmmmmm,' he said, 'nice here in the sun. But it won't get us lunch. While I'm away the mice will play. Or we might have rat. Or sparrow. What d'you fancy, Giglamps?'

'Chuck steak, laddie,' said Giglamps in a faraway voice, 'finely chopped, with a small piece of calf's liver on the side.' He ran his tongue neatly over the end of his nose.

'Or perhaps a little cod. Lightly steamed. With just the hint of a cheese sauce. And a saucer of Gold Top.'

'You've been dreaming,' said Tom.

'Och, it's staring up the street that does it, laddie,' said Giglamps, yawning. 'I can still see it just as it was. Humans everywhere. With their shopping baskets. Catering for our needs. Ah, humans! They were useful creatures to keep, you know. They've been gone a long time.'

The two friends lay silent, remembering those strange days. Usually no more than a handful of people visited the island in the season, but suddenly, over a couple of days, a great fleet of boats had

come from the mainland, boats of every size and kind, boats crammed with frightened, worried humans to swell the island's population from fifty or sixty to a thousand. They remembered how the grocer had run out of tinned food, and the baker of bread, and the greengrocer of fruit and vegetables, and the colonel of patience, and the vicar of hope. Every last pig, bullock, cow, calf, sheep, horse even, had made its way through Percy J. Plug's slaughterhouse and down one or another of a thousand throats. Until at last there was no meat on the island for humans to eat.

'And then that great ship came,' said Tom, picking up the other's train of thought as cats can.

'That's right,' said Giglamps, 'and they all had to wade out, among the rocks, carrying their bairns.'

'Took their dogs of course.'

'Stupid beasties, actually seemed to like swimming.'

'I wasn't going to get my feet wet.'

'Nor I.'

Gradually, as time passed after the going of the humans, the cats of the island had dropped into the habit of assuming amongst themselves their late owners' titles. The head of the cat family up at the Big House, for example, was always addressed as 'Colonel Bampton-Bush', the seniors at the island's three farms as 'Farmer Truebody', 'Farmer Goodfellow' and 'Farmer Sturdy', and the patriarch in the old rambling house beside the church was of course 'Vicar' to all. Only Tom used Giglamps' private name. To the rest he was 'Doctor'.

As for Tom himself, the island cats spoke of him as 'the Mouse Butcher'. It was a long time, after all, since the walls of Percy J. Plug's slaughterhouse had rung to the squeal of a dying pig, so that this title seemed right. Certainly the mice thought so, those that were left.

'What was it all about, d'you suppose?' Tom said.

'I don't know, laddie,' said Giglamps. 'I doubt we shall ever know. They were funny creatures, humans, you see. Always fighting. Always falling out, one lot with another lot. Many a time in the old days I've lain in the Doctor's room and listened to him and the Colonel and the Vicar discussing the strange habits of the human race.'

'Why did they fight?'

'Och, didn't like each other's ways. Often wanted to take the other lot's land.'

Tom looked shocked. 'Take over territory that wasn't theirs?' he said.

Giglamps nodded. 'They didn't seem to have any proper rules of behaviour like we do,' he said. 'About the only thing they were any good at was providing food on time,' and he looked sideways at his young friend.

The Mouse Butcher took the hint and jumped off the marble slab on to the dusty floor in one beautiful black sinuous movement. He slipped through the cat-flap (squeaky now for want of oil) in the back door of the shop, and padded soundlessly away down the weedy path through the wild garden.

Some minutes later, as he lay in ambush beside a runway, his eyes, ears, nose and muscles were all concentrated on the mouse to come, but his mind was running on the recent conversation. Fancy humans coveting each other's territory! No self-respecting cat would dream of such a thing!

Though I wouldn't mind a change from mice, he thought.

It was a simple four-course lunch. It was mouse for starters, with mouse to follow, then mouse, and mouse to finish. As always, Tom laid the four corpses neatly upon the marble slab in the window of the butcher's shop. It was as though he was impelled to in memory of Percy J. Plug, who had always so carefully arranged cutlet and chop, sirloin and brisket, liver and kidneys to catch the eye of the passer-by.

As they were about to begin, Tom saw that there was indeed a passer-by, both of whose great golden eyes were firmly caught by the sight of the outstretched mice.

'Who's the hungry-looking geezer outside?' he said.

'Geezer?' said Giglamps with a low purr of laughter. 'Good job he can't hear you. Frightfully posh chap that, you know. Persian. Pedigree as long as your tail.'

'Funny,' said Tom, 'I've never seen him before.'

'Well you wouldn't have, with all due respect, laddie,' said Giglamps. 'That's the Colonel. From up at the Big House. There's quite a few of them up there. That's the head of the family, Bertram Bampton-Bush. Never seen him down in the village before, they've always kept themselves very much to themselves.'

'You'd have thought the humans who used to live there would have taken them along,' Tom said. 'Pampered variety like that.'

'Och well, it was a curious set-up at the Big House,' said Giglamps. 'The cats belonged to the old fellow there but his wife had a lot of dogs, little fluffy yappy things. And no doubt he was told to save the dogs and leave the cats.'

'Told?' said Tom. 'D'you mean he just tamely did whatever his wife said?'

'Och yes, that's the way with a lot of humans. You'd not have been surprised if you'd known her. Her word was law. She was a Lady, daughter of a Duke.'

Tom had no idea what a Duke was, but he felt quite sure no wife of his would ever push him around like that. He looked again at the figure outside the window.

'Poor fellow,' he said. 'He looks ever so ribby.'

'Yes, well, they're probably finding it hard going,' said Giglamps. 'Always been spoon-fed, y'know. Never had to fend for themselves.'

'That reminds me,' said Tom, straight-faced, 'do start, please. I hope two will be enough for you?'

At the end of lunch, there only remained four pairs of back legs and four tails.

Outside the colonel sat still, seemingly hypnotised by the scene within. His coat was a beautiful smoky blue, the colour of lavender in a cottage garden, but it was harsh and staring.

Tom was a kind-hearted animal and it worried him to see a handsome cat in such a condition.

'I think I'll have a word with him,' he said. 'I might be able to help him.'

'Suit yourself,' said Giglamps, 'but he'll probably snub you. He's a very toffee-nosed fellow.'

What I mean is, he thought to himself, he's quality and you're common, good friend though you are. He belched quietly and yawned.

'Anyway, Tom, I must get home. Lot of work to do. I've got mice in the dispensary.'

'Of course,' said Tom, 'I know how conscientious you are about keeping things as they used to be.'

What I mean is, he thought to himself, old Doctor Macdonald would probably have been fast asleep in his armchair by this time in the afternoon, and that's just where you're going, lazybones, good friend though you are.

After the squeak of the cat-flap had announced Giglamps' departure, Tom neatly picked up the remains of the meal and made his way out. He turned round the side of the shop and walked up the narrow alleyway that separated it from the bakery next door. He came out on to the village street and dropped the legs and tails into the gutter. He sat for a moment, cleaning his nose and lips with the side of one forepaw and considering how to address such a very important Persian.

He was saved the trouble however; for the blue cat called out to him in a high and haughty voice, 'One moment, my good cat. I'd like a word with you.'

Stuck-up beast, thought Tom, and he got up and walked, slowly and deliberately, towards the other, his ears pricked, his tail high, his green eyes fixed on a spot somewhere just above the blue head.

There was no actual threat in the manner of his approach but for all that it made the Colonel uncomfortable. Maybe it was Tom's appearance, sleek, fit, hard-muscled, but at all events the blue back arched a little, the blue tail fluffed out, and the high voice climbed a fraction higher.

'Now look here, I don't want any nonsense from you, my good cat,' said the Persian in a slightly trembly tone.

'I haven't any nonsense to offer you,' said Tom pleasantly, and he stopped a yard away and sat down.

'Now look here,' said the other, 'you don't seem to know who I am.'

'Haven't a clue.'

'Well, I'm Bampton-Bush. Bertram Bampton-Bush.'

'Plug,' said Tom.

'Now look here, Plug,' said Bertram Bampton-Bush, 'I just happened to notice you, er, lunching with Macdonald. Decent enough sort of animal in his way. You seemed to be providing the food. I take it he employs you, what?'

Just as I thought, said Tom to himself, he's half starved for all his airs and graces. There could be something in this for me.

'We have an arrangement,' he said. 'After all, gentlecats can't be expected to do their own hunting the way we common fellows do.'

'Well, I'd hardly call Macdonald a . . .'

'Especially,' interrupted Tom, 'a real aristocat like yourself, Sir,' he added quietly. A quick glance from the green eyes saw the golden ones widen in pleasure and the flat snub-nosed face look even more self-satisfied.

'Ah. Quite,' said Bertram. 'Well. Now look here, Plug my good cat. I think I can see my way, as a special favour to you that is, to putting a little business in your path. How would you like to supply me and my family, up at the Big House?'

Tom was not prepared to allow the Persian to believe that Giglamps was his only 'customer'.

'I'm a busy cat, you know, Colonel Bampton-Bush,' he said. 'I have a great many calls on my time. Catering for you would mean my taking on extra help. I imagine you have a large family?'

'I have a wife,' said Bertram. 'And about a dozen children or more.'

'Exactly,' said Tom. 'And you're probably thinking of a daily delivery?'

'Certainly,' said Bertram. 'You see, Plug, it's not simply a case of people of my sort not caring much for working-cats' pursuits. Mousing. Ratting. That sort of thing. All right for some, I dare say. And as you rightly remark, one is used to being fed on a decent dish with decent food from the fridge. But it's not simply that.'

'What then?' said Tom, though he knew the answer.

'Well, the fact is, Plug, that the humans were extremely wasteful creatures, always dropping bits of food under tables and leaving it around on plates in cupboards and chucking it to their damned dogs. And since they left, there's been no waste food in the Big House. So the mice and rats have left too. There's nothing for us to eat.'

Oh yes there is, thought Tom. Out in the countryside, where the last corn crops re-germinate and the root crops still sit in the ground and the wild fruits and berries drop – there's food for a million rodents and birds, animals that any cat worth his salt can go and catch for himself. You may not be worth your salt, Colonel B-B, but perhaps you could be useful to me. I'm not saying I want to take over your territory like humans apparently do, he thought. But I wouldn't mind a good look round it.

'I quite understand, sir,' he said smoothly. 'I'm sure we can work something out. Can you think of anything you might care to give me

in return for my services? For example, if you have sources of food supply up there not available to common or garden cats, I could perhaps contract to butcher them for you and your family on the understanding that I should receive a proportion for my own use?'

The golden eyes glinted in the flat face. 'Now look here, Plug,' said Bertram Bampton-Bush, 'I believe you're on to something there. I mean, one doesn't actually go out on to the estate, you know – too damned muddy and brambly – but one of my sons is pally with young Tibby Truebody down at the Home Farm – boys will be boys, y'know – and she told him that the place is thick with pheasant and partridge. And of course, there are quite a lot of rabbits. And hares. If you can catch them. Ha ha.'

'Ha ha,' said Tom, and the green eyes glinted in the sharp face. There was more talk and a meeting at the Big House was arranged for the next day. Then they made their good-byes.

Once Tom was out of sight, he doubled back and watched from hiding. And as he watched, the high and mighty Colonel Bertram, head of the family of Bampton-Bush, lord of the Big House, the aristocat of the island, looked hastily around him, crept quickly forward and bolted the legs and tails. He peered around again, and then drew himself to his full height and with the dignity of centuries of good breeding, set off up the village street to the Big House.

Almost in the middle of the island was a huge deep pit, perhaps the size of a football stadium. Over centuries men had made it, digging there for red marl to spread upon their fields. But for the last hundred years, it had fallen out of use and become overgrown, not just with thick undergrowth and scrub but with tall trees. Their tops were now level with the rim of the marl-pit, so that a watcher on the edge would have looked down into a great sea of greenery at every level.

The islanders had called it Hobbs' Hole, for an old poacher named Billy Hobbs had once lived there in a hut of sticks and corrugated iron and sacks. Billy Hobbs and his hut were long gone, but Hobbs' Hole was as full of wild things as it had been in his day. In the middle of it was a hollow oak tree. And in the middle of the tree sat the wildest thing of all.

At first sight you would have thought this creature too big to be a cat, and at second glance too hideous, for what he gained in size was balanced by a saga of losses. One ear was in tatters, the other almost gone. He had but one eye, and an injury to his great round face had pulled up one side of his mouth in a permanent snarl. A trap had removed all the toes from one forefoot. His tail was a stump.

This was Great Mog.

Great Mog was a feral cat, a cat gone wild. He had been born in the village, the only surviving child of a thin half-starved female who belonged to nobody in particular. She had taken to stealing to support herself and her kitten. Principally she hung about Percy J. Plug's shop and it was here one day that the incident occurred which was to alter the shape of both Great Mog's life and his person.

One afternoon when he was about two months old, Mog accompanied his mother to the butcher's shop. She waited in the alleyway between it and the bakery, her anxious pointed head poking around the corner to watch for a suitable moment, while behind her the tabby tom-kitten fidgeted impatiently.

When at last they reached the door the shop was empty of people but full of the heavenly smell of meat. The mother made for a string of sausages upon the slab, the child for a clutch of kidneys of one of the tables, when out from the back room came the butcher, cleaver in hand, dog at heel! The young Mog's last sight of his wretched mother was of her frantic fleeing form barely a cat's length in front of the yellow lurcher's long jaws, before he turned to see the butcher towering above him, arm upraised. Down whistled the shining cleaver, thudding into the scoured surface of the wooden table, and then Percy J. Plug had his shop to himself again.

But between the pork chops and the pigs' kidneys lay three tabby inches of kitten tail.

And so out into the wild went the orphan Mog, to learn to hunt and to kill and to survive. By some freak of heredity, his bob-tailed body grew to giant size, and with it, as traps and shot-guns and dogs made their contributions to his looks, grew his hatred of all living things. All his memories made the outlaw bitter, but especially the memory of that day in the butcher's shop.

On this particular evening Great Mog sat in his leafy nest in the crown of the hollow tree and looked about him. You could not say his ears were pricked – there was not enough of them – but he was listening intently to the noises in Hobbs' Hole. He had nothing to fear, since men and their dogs were gone, but he had a territory to protect, for the marl-pit was his, and his alone. Between it and the village and farms was a kind of no-cat's-land, where others might hunt if they wished but woe betide them if they were rash enough to enter the Hole. Once, two cats from an outlying farm had indeed ventured in, but they did not live to regret their rashness. Great Mog killed them both, and the magpies and the ants cleaned up.

But strangely there was one cat that had the right of entry, perhaps because he was of use to the great wild tabby, perhaps because he was so mean and insignificant in appearance. He was a very thin small brown cat, so small he could have walked under Great Mog's belly had he been fool enough. His pointed face and slanting almond eyes came from some Siamese ancestor. He was quick, and servile, and cunning. His name was Creep.

This evening Great Mog could hear a whole orchestra of sounds.

Above and around him were the noises of bird-song and animal scamperings. He heard the slow rustle of a foraging hedgehog, the grunts of badgers coming out of their sett deep in the red marl, the pattering footsteps of a fox passing beneath the hollow tree on his way out to the night's hunting.

Great Mog stretched and yawned and was just about to climb down from his nest when a thin nasal voice made him spin round.

'Evenin', Captain,' said Creep. 'Hope I didn't startle you.' Great Mog's expression could not change, for his snarl was fixed, but his one eye flashed and the stump of his tail twitched.

'Damn you, Creep,' he spat. 'Told you a dozen times. Don't come in upwind. Bad for my nerves.'

'Nerves, Captain?' said Creep. 'Why, you 'aven't got a nerve in that whole magnificent body of yours. Ain't nothing on this island could scare you.' He crouched very flat, ready for instant flight, his slit-eyes fixed on the monster above.

Great Mog came down from his tree, a little awkwardly because of the missing claws on his forefoot. He sat on his haunches with his back to the little brown cat and combed his ragged ears with his good paw.

'Well?' he said. 'What d'you want? Eh?'

'Want, Captain? Me, Captain?' whined Creep. 'Why, just the pleasure of settin' eyes on you . . .'

'Get on with it,' cut in Great Mog, in a low growl.

They knew each other well, these two, hated each other but used each other. The one valued his right of entry to Hobbs' Hole and the status it gave him in the eyes of the rest of the island's cats. They did not know exactly what it was that lived in those green leafy depths, but there were tales of ghosts, and mother cats frightened naughty kittens with threats of the monster of the marl-pit. All gave Creep a wide berth. The other relied upon him for news of anything and everything that might go on in the outside world, that is to say in the island outside Hobbs' Hole. Quick, silent, small, cunning, Creep was the perfect spy.

He saw the twitching stump and tensed himself for flight should the wild cat's temper boil over, as it often did.

'Sorry, Captain,' he said hastily. 'It was just something I saw today in the village. Thought it might interest you.'

'Men?' said Mog quickly. 'Are men back?'

'Niaouw!' said Creep. 'Niaouw, nothing like that, Captain. It was just two cats having a chat.'

'What's funny about that?'

'One of them was the Colonel.'

'Down in the village?' said Mog. 'I thought you told me that chicken-and-cream lot never went outside the Big House?'

'Exactly,' said Creep, 'but there he was. All skin and bone, too. Eating rubbish out of the gutter.'

'Who was the other then?'

Now Creep knew everything about everything. He knew how Great Mog had lost both mother and tail. All right, he thought, the man and his dog have been gone for ages but there's a black cat living in the old shop, the Mouse Butcher they call him. Can't even have been born when old grumbleguts here got the chop but that won't matter. Let's have some fun. Let's stir up some trouble. Let's see if we can make the fur fly!

'The other one, Captain?' he said. 'Oh, that was the cat from the butcher's shop.'

'Butcher's shop?' said Great Mog very softly, and his one eye flashed and his stump began to twitch.

'Oh, didn't you know?' said Creep carelessly. 'There's a black cat lives in the shop. Tom Plug his name is but everyone calls him the Mouse Butcher.'

'The Mouse Butcher,' said Mog in a kind of thick whisper. 'Did he belong to . . . that man?' His stump fluttered madly.

'Yes.'

A listener might have thought there was at least one great dog left upon the island, such was the deep growling that mingled with the bird-song in Hobbs' Hole. At last it died away, and Great Mog spoke again, still quietly.

'What were they saying?' he asked. 'Could you hear?'

'Niaouw, Captain,' said Creep. 'I couldn't get close enough.'

'Find out,' said Great Mog. 'And now get out.'

And as Creep made his silent way up the steep side of the pit he heard beneath him the horrid rasping noise of Great Mog sharpening the claws of his good foot on the hollow tree.

The morning after his meeting with Bertram Bampton-Bush, Tom Plug made his way, as arranged to the Big House. Like all cats, he was intensely curious, and he could hardly wait to set foot in those spacious grounds where, in the old days, he would never have dreamed of going. So he arrived extremely early, and, finding no one about, allowed himself the luxury of a good look round. He toured the walled kitchen garden, a jungle of weeds now, and searched the long dry greenhouses, empty save for the skeletons of dead chrysanthemums. Then he slipped through a broken door set in the wall and across the tall grasses of what had been a sweep of lawn to the once formal gardens.

There was a pattern of symmetrical flower beds – now covered in groundsel and dandelions – triangles, diamonds, oblongs, quarter-circles, each bounded by a ragged hedge of box. In the centre of this pattern was a large round pond. Pausing to lap, Tom could see below his reflection a number of huge golden fish, moving slowly among the water-lily stems.

Suddenly he felt that he was being watched and looked quickly up at the dozen or so square eyes that were the front windows of the Big House. They were blank – or was that a movement at the corner of one of them?

Next instant there was the most terrible blood-chilling shriek behind him that laid Tom's black ears flat and set every nerve in him a-jangle. Tail held straight out behind him, he shot across the grass-grown gravel paths and in through the first window that offered, while behind him a peacock strolled majestically down for his morning drink.

As Tom lay breathless on the floor of the room into which he had burst he heard someone giggling – or the nearest a cat can get to a giggle, a kind of soft purr with a hiccup in it – behind a dusty sofa. And in a moment there walked out from behind it the most beautiful creature Tom had ever seen. Scarcely more than a kitten, she had the flattest face, the blackest nose, the dearest little whiskers, the most glorious golden eyes, and her coat – her long soft exquisite coat – was the most wonderful shade of the most wonderful blue that Tom could possibly have imagined in the world, a world turned instantly into Paradise.

Walking forward – in, of course, the most unbelievably elegant way – she sat down in front of the black intruder, and the gold eyes looked directly into the green.

'You're a very fast runner,' said this vision of beauty – in a voice like cream and treacle mixed.

Tom gulped.

'Got to keep fit,' he growled awkwardly.

'You look *very* fit,' she said. 'By the way, introduce yourself.'

'Tom,' said Tom. 'I mean my name's Tom Plug. The Mouse Butcher.'

'Oh,' said the vision. 'Sorry. I'm Diana. Diana Bampton-Bush. I live here. So I think you'd better tell me what you want, Mr Tom Plug.'

'I've got an appointment,' said Tom. 'To see your . . .' He was just going to say 'father' when it occurred to him that she might possibly be not a daughter but – oh horrors! – a very young wife. He became thoroughly confused.

'To see, er Colonel Bampton,' he said, 'that is, I mean, Colonel Bertram-Bush.'

Diana's golden eyes positively twinkled.

'You want to see Daddy?' she said.

Tom heaved a huge inward sigh of relief. 'Yes,' he said. 'Yes, please, miss.'

'Oh for goodness sake!' she said. 'Call me Di. Everybody does. Except Mummy.'

Tom was too bewitched to ask what Mummy called her, but the answer came that very instant. From the depths of the house came a loud commanding voice echoing along the lengthy corridors and around the high-ceilinged rooms.

'Di-*ah*-na!' it cried. 'Di-*ah*-na!'

Then suddenly the room filled with Blue Persians, youngsters of Diana's age, perhaps her litter-mates, and a number of young adults, a dozen or more in all. They crouched or sat, and stared unblinkingly at the black stranger. And then through them swept the figure of Lady Maud. Like her husband's, her coat was dull and matted. Round her scrawny neck was the tattered remnant of a red silk bow, and she was painfully thin.

Behind her came Bertram, and it was easy to see that the parents had been giving almost all the food they could find to their family, at their own expense.

'Di-ah-na,' said Lady Maud. 'Who, pray, is this, ah, visitah?'

'This is Mr Plug, Mummy,' said Diana quickly. 'The Mouse Butcher.'

'Butchah?' said Lady Maud, on a rising note.

'Yes, he's come to see Daddy on business.'

'On business? To see your Fathah? There must be some errah.'

'No, no, Di is quite right, my dear,' said Bertram hastily in a placatory voice. 'Come along Plug, my good fellow, come into my

study and we'll have a chat,' and he turned and went hastily out of the room and along a corridor.

Tom hesitated before the baleful stare of the lady of the house, but Di gave him a little tap with one adorably rounded paw. 'Go on, Tom,' she whispered, and Tom, his mind reeling at the touch and the sound of his name on her lips, pushed his way through the serried Persian ranks and followed the Colonel.

The deal was soon struck. Bertram Bampton-Bush was no business cat. Tom was. Bertram was a soft touch. Tom a hard nut. Bertram was half-starved, as was his wife, and his family soon would be he feared, unless someone could be found with the strength and skills to provide for them. Tom, it seemed, was that someone, and Bertram gave in to every condition that Tom set.

'I shall need a free run over your entire estate, Colonel Bampton-Bush,' said Tom.

'Yes.'

'That freedom of entry to apply to any cats I may have working for me.'

'Yes, yes.'

'In return I will contract to provide you and your family with the choicest available foodstuffs, all you can possibly eat.'

Bertram passed his tongue rapidly around his lips. 'Very well. Plug.'

'And over and above that,' said Tom, 'I shall be entitled to the balance of all kills for my own use. As I seem to remember, you agreed to this at our first meeting?'

'A proportion, I think you said, Plug.'

'The balance.'

'Oh, very well.'

Tom thought quickly. If I'm to see Di regularly, he said to himself, I must have the right of access to the Big House, so that we can meet often. He had no intention of revealing the reason for his final demand, either to Bertram then or to Giglamps in conversation later, but like a boxer who sees his opponent reeling, he decided to go for the knock-out blow.

'One last thing, sir,' he said. 'If I'm to serve you properly I must have a room in your house for my own use.'

Bertram gulped. 'My wife . . .' he began.

But Tom went easily on. 'You see, there's little point in my having to take your family's share, the very choicest as I said, all the way down to my shop in the village and then bring it back here again, now is there? I mean, far more convenient for you if I butchered it here – you'll want it all properly prepared of course, a gentlecat like you.'

Bertram gulped again. 'I'm not sure that my wife would be, will . . .'

'I do hope you'll see your way to agreeing to this last point, sir,' interrupted Tom sweetly. 'Otherwise . . .'

'No, no, Plug,' said Bertram hastily, 'certainly . . . you must have a room . . . Can see that . . . The, er, servants' quarters . . . Er, self-contained little wing . . . Sure you wouldn't mind, good fellow like you . . ? My wife . . .' He finished lamely, his eyes filled with pleading.

'Of course, sir,' said Tom. 'The servants' quarters will do admirably.'

Nine, ten, out! he said to himself.

Giglamps heard all this later that evening, after supper. They had shared a pheasant.

'He was just strolling down the drive as I left the Big House,' Tom said. 'Practically walked into my mouth. They're not used to being hunted, you see.'

Giglamps cleaned his face delicately, belched luxuriously and settled himself comfortably in the deep leather armchair.

'Mah-vellous!' he said. 'Pah-fectly mah-vellous!'

'That's it!' chuckled Tom. 'That's Lady Maud's voice exactly! How did you know?'

'Oh well, I have met her, laddie. Once. In the old days. Doctor Macdonald used to go up to the Big House quite regularly to play some card game with Colonel and Lady B-B and the Vicar. On one occasion I followed him and slipped in, uninvited. Never again though.'

'Why, what happened?'

'Well, I think old Bertram was prepared to be civil, you know, offer me a small saucer of milk, that sort of thing. He's a stuffy old snob, but basically kind-hearted. But her Ladyship wasn't having any of it.

I remember she was lying in front of a fire in one of the smaller rooms, looking absolutely magnificent, one must say, with a brilliant red silk bow tied round her neck. And when her husband had introduced me she looked not at me but straight through me, and said in that awful braying voice, "Some othah time, perhaps, Bertie. It's very neahly time for dinnah, and you're not dressed yet. I'm sure Mr, ah, Macdonald can find his own way out." And off I went like a cuffed kitten.'

There was a long easy silence while the two friends lay contentedly in a brilliant sea of black and bronze and green feathers, thinking pleasant thoughts.

At last Giglamps belched once more and said, 'That was a meal and a half, Tom. Get some of that into Bertram and Lady Maud and in a little while they'll give you anything you want.'

A vision rose before Tom's eyes – a vision with the flattest face, the blackest nose, the dearest little whiskers, the most glorious golden eyes.

'I hope they will, Gig,' he said. 'I hope they will.'

Tom spent the night at Giglamps' house. Breakfast next morning was less luxurious, just a couple of sparrows.

'Sorry,' Tom said after an early hunt, 'that's all I could find. Anyway a bird in the hand . . .'

'. . . is worth two in the Bampton-Bush,' said Giglamps. 'Ha ha.'

Giglamps licked his lips, brushed his whiskers out, left, right, and regarded his friend straightly. 'I can see what's in it for you,' he said. 'Good hunting and the best of grub. But it'll be hard work, you know. All the killing, the carrying, the butchering. You're going to need help.'

'Oh thanks, Giglamps, that's decent of you.'

'What? No, no, I mean expert help.'

Tom scratched his head with one hindpaw. 'Well, I don't know where I'm going to get it. The farm cats are too far out, and as for the village cats, who is there? You tell me. There's half a dozen cottage cats, and that old pair from the pub, Rose and Crown, but not a decent hunter amongst them. Talk about pulling down a pheasant or a hare, most of them must have their work cut out to catch a mouse! When all's said and done, "Mouse is the staff of life"! As Ecclesiastes would say,' he added.

They looked at each other.

'That's your cat, laddie!' said Giglamps, grinning as though he'd come straight from Cheshire.

'Of course! Of course! That's it!' cried Tom excitedly, 'Ecclesiastes and his family. The most expert specialist mousers on the island. If it's patience that's wanted, they've got in, especially that boy Job.'

Ecclesiastes' family was numerous and as poor as the church-mice they lived on.

'Look,' said Giglamps. 'Why don't I go down and have a word with Ecclesiastes? I mean he's an old friend of mine, whereas I think you hardly know him?'

'You mean he's *your* sort of cat,' said Tom with a smile, 'and I'm a bit common.'

'No, no,' said Giglamps. 'Of course not.'

'Well, I don't like to put you to all that trouble,' said Tom. 'Walking all the way down to the Vicarage' (it was a good two hundred yards), 'straight after breakfast.'

'You mean you're young and active,' said Giglamps with a smile, 'and I'm a fat old lazybones.'

'No no,' said Tom. 'Of course not.'

Giglamps went straight to the churchyard. It was a fine morning, and he found what he had expected. By almost every grave, it seemed, there lurked a cat. They were of all sizes, and of all colours, but they had in common a certain look a kind of tired resignation to a life of hard work and small rewards. Still as the statues of angels and cherubim above them, the innumerable family of Ecclesiastes waited, by headstone and by footstone, by monument and memorial, for fortune to give them that day their daily mouse.

Giglamps, puffing a little from the unaccustomed exercise, rested a moment in the long grass looking all about him for the head of the family. Eventually, espying a sudden movement beneath a great yew tree in a distant corner, he trotted down and found the patriarch, his paws together in an attitude of prayer, and between them an extremely small shrew.

'Morning Vicar,' said Giglamps. 'Caught you red-handed, eh? How about the sixth commandment, then?'

He always said this and always Ecclesiastes made the same reply.

'Needs must, my dear Doctor,' he said, 'when the Devil drives.'

Mercifully, he ended the shrew's feeble struggles with one quick bite, and rose to his feet.

Ecclesiastes was a tall thin cat of mournful appearance, dark grey, with a broad collar of white fur around his neck. His sole wealth lay in his voice which was rich and rounded and resonant.

'Dear friend,' he boomed, 'tell me, I pray, to what happy chance do I owe the undoubted pleasure of your company?'

'"Happy chance" is right," said Giglamps and he proceeded to explain Tom's need for assistance in his new venture.

'I suggested this approach to you and your family, Ecclesiastes,' he concluded, 'because you are such expert hunters and because there are, if you'll forgive me, so many of you. How many are there, in fact?'

'A multitude,' said Ecclesiastes. 'Sometimes, if you in turn, dear friend, will forgive me, providing for them seems to necessitate as great a miracle as the Feeding of the Five Thousand. In fact, not counting myself or my dear wife, who has remained at the Vicarage with the seven latest arrivals, there are a score and ten of us at work here this morning. It is the habit of my family, as I think you know, to choose our children's names from the books of the Old Testament, but at the rate of increase with which we are blessed, we shall soon be using the New.'

'All the more reason,' said Giglamps, 'for Tom's offer to be of interest to you.'

'Verily,' said Ecclesiastes. 'Let us repair to the Vicarage. I must, in all things, consult my wife.'

They made their soft-footed way between the moss-covered tombs and the weatherworn gravestones, the only movements beside their own a number of sudden pounces from one or other of Ecclesiastes' silent, watchful children. At each the patriarch voiced his approval, lowering his voice to a mere purr.

'Well done, Leviticus,' he murmured. 'Oh, neatly, neatly, Habbakuk! See, a bold jump from Exodus! (An outgoing boy, that,' he whispered proudly to Giglamps.) 'Ah, Lamentations has missed. How sad.'

Inside the Vicarage, cold and damp even in such weather, they found Ecclesiastes' wife, a tubby tabby person, surrounded by a cluster of tumbling kittens. Unlike the rest of her family and despite the trials and tribulations of a life of penury and thirty-seven children, she gave an impression of comfortable jolliness. Her name was Genesis.

'So you see, my dear,' finished Ecclesiastes, after a short sermon, 'it appears that, thanks to Mr Plug's offer, we may look forward to better times.'

'Land of milk and honey,' said Giglamps.

'Super!' said Genesis. 'Simply super! Really most frightfully grateful to you, Doctor. Be such a change. So jolly fed up with always eating the same thing.'

Ecclesiastes threw back his head and raised his fine voice. 'Cat shall not live by mouse alone!' he cried.

Dick King-Smith

(b.1922)

Dick King-Smith enjoyed several careers before becoming a full-time writer in 1982, when he was 60. Between 1941 and 1946, he served in the British Army with the famous Grenadier Guards regiment. Afterwards, he spent twenty years as a farmer in Gloucestershire and a further seven years as a primary school teacher. Since beginning his writing career, Dick King-Smith has produced a children's book almost every year and sometimes more than one. He is the creator of Magnus Powermouse.

THE NEW NOAH

Gerald Durrell has collected animals for his Jersey zoo from all over the world. Among many other animals he came across in Africa, Cholmondeley, the sophisticated chimp, was a particular favourite, due to his endearing habits and remarkable intelligence.

When Cholmondely, the chimpanzee, joined the collection, he immediately became the uncrowned king of it, not only because of his size, but also because he was so remarkably intelligent. Cholmondely had been the pet of a District Officer who, wanting to send the ape to the London zoo, and hearing that I was collecting wild animals in that region and would shortly be returning to England, wrote and asked me if I would mind taking Cholmondely with me and handing him over to the zoo authorities. I wrote back to say that, as I already had a large collection of monkeys, another chimpanzee would not make any difference, so I would gladly escort Cholmondely back to England. I imagined that he would be quite a young chimp, perhaps two years old, and standing about two feet high. When he arrived I got a considerable shock.

A small van drew up outside the camp one morning and in the back of it was an enormous wooden crate. It was big enough, I thought, to house an elephant. I wondered what on earth could be inside, and when the driver told me that it contained Cholmondely I remember thinking how silly his owner was to send such a small chimpanzee in such a huge crate. I opened the door and looked inside and there sat Cholmondely. One glance at him and I realized that this was no baby chimpanzee but a fully grown one about eight or nine years old. Sitting hunched up in the dark crate, he looked as though he were about twice as big as me, and from the expression on his face I gathered that the trip had not been to his liking. Before I could shut the door of the box, however, Cholmondely had extended a long, hairy arm, clasped my hand in his and shaken it warmly. Then he turned round and gathered up a great length of chain (one end of which was fastened to a collar round his neck), draped it carefully over his arm, and stepped down, out of the box. He stood there for a moment and, after surveying me carefully, examined the camp with great interest, where upon he held out his hand, looking at me inquiringly. I took it in mine and we walked into the marquee together.

Cholmondely immediately went and seated himself on one of the chairs by the camp table, dropped his chain on the floor and sat back and crossed his legs. He gazed round the tent for a few minutes with a rather supercilious expression on his face, and evidently deciding that it would do he turned and looked at me inquiringly again. Obviously, he wanted me to offer him something after his tiring journey. I had been warned before he arrived that he was a hardened tea drinker, and so I called out to the cook and told him to make a pot of tea. Then I went out and had a look in Cholmondely's crate, and in the bottom

I found an enormous and very battered tin mug. When I returned to the tent with this, Cholmondely was quite overjoyed and even praised me for my cleverness in finding it, by uttering a few cheerful 'hoo hoo' noises.

While we were waiting for the tea to arrive, I sat down opposite Cholmondely and lit a cigarette. To my surprise, he became very excited and held out his hand across the table to me. Wondering what he would do, I handed him the cigarette packet. He opened it, took out a cigarette and put it between his lips. He then reached out his hand again and I gave him the matches; to my astonishment, he took one out of the box, struck it, lit his cigarette and threw the box down on the table. Lying back in his chair he blew out clouds of smoke in the most professional manner. No one had told me that Cholmondely smoked. I wondered rather anxiously what other bad habits he might have which his master had not warned me about.

Just at that moment, the tea was brought in and Cholmondely greeted its appearance with loud and expressive hoots of joy. He

watched me carefully while I half-filled his mug with milk and then added the tea. I had been told that he had a very sweet tooth, so I put in six large spoons of sugar, an action which he greeted with grunts of satisfaction. He placed his cigarette on the table and seized the mug with both hands; then he stuck out his lower lip very carefully and dipped it into the tea to make sure it was not too hot. As it was a trifle warm, he sat there blowing on it vigorously until it was cool enough, and then he drank it all down without stopping once. When he had drained the last drops, he peered into the mug and scooped out all the sugar he could with his forefinger. After that, he tipped the mug up on his nose and sat with it like that for about five minutes until the very last of the sugar had trickled down into his mouth.

I had Cholmondely's big box placed some distance away from the marquee, and fixed the end of his chain to a large tree stump. He was too far away, I thought, to make a nuisance of himself but near enough to be able to watch everything that went on and to conduct long conversations with me in his 'hoo hoo' language. But on the day of his arrival he caused trouble almost as soon as I had fixed him to his tree stump. Outside the marquee was a lot of small tame monkeys tied on long strings attached to stakes driven into the ground. They were about ten in number, and over them I had constructed a palm leaf roof as a shelter from the sun. As Cholmondely was examining his surroundings, he noticed these monkeys, some eating fruit and others lying in the sun, and decided he would have a little under-arm bowling practice. I was working inside the marquee when all at once I heard the most terrific uproar going on outside. The monkeys were screaming and chattering with rage, and I rushed out to see what had

happened. Cholmondely, apparently, had picked up a rock the size of a cabbage and hurled it at the smaller monkeys, luckily missing them all, but frightening them out of their wits. If one of them had been hit by such a big rock, it would have been killed instantly.

Just as I arrived on the scene, Cholmondely had picked up another stone and was swinging it backwards and forwards like a professional cricketer, taking better aim. He was annoyed at having missed all the monkeys with his first shot. I grabbed a stick and hurried towards him, shouting, and, to my surprise Cholmondely dropped the rock and put his arms over his head, and started to roll on the ground and scream. In my haste, I had picked up a very small twig and this made no impression on him at all, for his back was as broad and as hard as a table.

I gave him two sharp cuts with this silly little twig and followed it up with a serious scolding. He sat there picking bits of leaf off his fur and looking very guilty. With the aid of the Africans, I set to work and cleared away all the rocks and stones near his box, and, giving him another scolding, went back to my work. I hoped that this telling-off might have some effect on him, but when I looked out of the marquee some time later, I saw him digging in the earth, presumably in search of more ammunition.

Not long after his arrival at the camp, Cholmondely, to my alarm, fell ill. For nearly two weeks he went off his food, refusing even the most tempting fruit and other delicacies, and even rejecting his daily ration of tea, a most unheard-of occurrence. All he had was a few sips of water every day, and gradually he grew thinner and thinner, his eyes sank into their sockets, and I really thought he was going to die.

BIRO

He lost all interest in life and sat hunched up in his box all day, with his eyes closed. It was very bad for him to spend all day moping in this fashion, so in the evenings, just before the sun went down, when it was cool, I used to make him come out for walks with me. These walks were only short, and we had to rest every few yards, for Cholmondely was weak with lack of food.

One evening, just before I took him out for a walk, I filled my pockets with a special kind of biscuit that he had been very fond of. We went slowly up to the top of a small hill just beyond the camp and then sat there to admire the view. As we rested, I took a biscuit out of my pocket and ate it, smacking my lips with enjoyment, but not offering any to Cholmondely. He looked very surprised, for he knew that I always shared my food with him when we were out together. I ate a second biscuit and he watched me closely to see if I enjoyed it as much as the first. When he saw that I did, he dipped his hand into my pocket, pulled out a biscuit, smelled it suspiciously, and then, to my delight, ate it up and started looking for another. I knew then that he was going to get better. The next morning he drank a mugful of sweet tea and ate seventeen biscuits, and for three days lived entirely on this diet. After this his appetite returned with a rush, and for the next fortnight he ate twice as much as he had ever done before, and cost me a small fortune in bananas.

There were only two things that Cholmondely disliked. One of them was the Africans and the other, snakes. I think that when he was a baby some Africans must have teased him. Whatever the reason, however, he certainly got his own back on more than one occasion. He would hide inside the box and wait until an African passed close by and then he would rush out with all his hair standing on end, swinging his long arms and screaming in the most terrifying manner. Many a fat African woman carrying a basket of fruit on her head would chance to pass too closely to Cholmondely's box, and would have to drop her basket, pick up her skirts and run for dear life, while Cholmondely danced victoriously at the end of his chain, hooting and showing all his teeth in a grin of delight.

With snakes, of course, he was not nearly so brave. If he saw me handling one, he would get very agitated, wringing his hands and moaning with fear, and if I put the reptile on the ground and it started to crawl towards him, he would run to the very end of his chain and scream loudly for help, throwing bits of stick and grass at the snake to try and stop it coming any closer.

One night, I went to shut him up in his box, as usual, and, to my surprise, he flatly refused to go into it. His bed of banana leaves was nicely made, and so I thought he was simply being naughty, but when I started to scold him, he took me by the hand, led me up to his box and left me there while he retreated to the safety of the end of his chain, and stood watching me anxiously. I realized there must be something inside, of which he was frightened, and when I cautiously investigated I found a very small snake coiled up in the centre of his bed. After I had captured it, I found that it was a harmless type; Cholmondely, of course, could not tell the difference, and he was taking no chances.

Cholmondely was so quick at learning tricks and so willing to show off that when he returned to England, he became quite famous and even made several appearances on television, delighting the audiences by sitting on a chair, with a hat on, taking a cigarette and lighting it for himself; pouring out and drinking a glass of beer and many other things. I think he must have become rather swollen-headed with his success, for not long after this he managed to escape from the zoo and went wandering off by himself through Regent's Park, much to the horror of everyone he met. On reaching the main road, he found a bus standing there and promptly climbed aboard, for he loved being taken for a ride. The passengers, however, decided they would rather not travel by that particular bus if Cholmondely was going to use it as well, and they were all struggling to get out when some keepers arrived from the zoo and took Cholmondely in charge. He was marched back to his cage in disgrace, but if I know Cholmondely, he must have thought it worth any amount of scoldings just for the sight of all those people trying to get off the bus together, and getting stuck in the door. Cholmondely had a great sense of humour.

Gerald Durrell

(b.1925)

Gerald Durrell is a zoologist and lives on Jersey, in the Channel Islands. He is deeply involved with the wild life of Jersey and has his own zoo there. In 1959, Gerald Durrell founded the Jersey Wildlife Preservation Trust, and his long experience with birds and animals has provided material for the many books he has written in the last 35 years.

BORN FREE

Joy Adamson and her husband George, live in a wildlife reserve in Kenya. They adopt Elsa, the lioness cub, and her two sisters, when their mother is killed. The other two cubs are sent away to a zoo in the Netherlands, but Joy keeps Elsa, and eventually decides to try to return her to the wild – an enterprise fraught with dangers, not least for the animal herself.

ELSA HAS CHARMING MANNERS at all times; no matter for how short a time we have been separated, she will greet us ceremoniously, walking from one to the other, rubbing her head against us while miaowing in a low moan. Invariably, I come first, then George, followed by Nuru, and whoever happens to be near is afterwards greeted in the same way. She knows at once who likes her and reacts affectionately. She tolerates justifiably nervous guests, but those who are really scared have a hard time. Not that she has ever done them any harm but she delights in thoroughly terrifying them.

Since she was a tiny cub she has known just how to use her weight. But now she had become much more effective. Whenever she wanted to stop us, she flung herself with all her force at our feet, pressing her body against our shins and thus knocking us over.

Soon after our return from a safari to Lake Rudolf when we took her out for her evening walks she began to display a growing restlessness. Sometimes she refused to return with us, and she spent the night out in the bush. Usually we succeeded in getting her back by going to fetch her in the Land-Rover. In fact, she soon decided that it was a waste of energy to walk home when a car had been specially brought to fetch her. So she would jump on to the canvas roof and loll at her ease, and from this vantage point she could watch out for game as we drove along. This was a very satisfactory arrangement from her point of view but, unfortunately, the manufacturers had not designed the roof as a couch for a lioness. As a result the supports began to give way under the strain and we found Elsa gradually subsiding on top of us. So George had to rig up extra supports and reinforce the canvas.

When she was not with us, Nuru was still always in charge of Elsa; one day we wanted to film him with her and told him that he should wear something rather smarter than his usual tattered shirt and trousers. In a few minutes he reappeared in a startling, close-fitting cream-coloured jacket, with braid and frogging down the front, which he had bought for his wedding. We thought that he looked just like a professional lion tamer in it. Elsa took one look at him and made at once for the bush; from there she peeped out from behind a shrub until she had established his identity. Then she came up to him and gave him a smack as though to say, 'What the devil do you mean by giving me such a fright?'

Nuru and Elsa had many adventures together; for instance, one day Nuru told us that while they were resting under a bush a leopard approached them down wind. Elsa watched eagerly and, although tense with excitement, kept still and controlled herself, except for her

tail, until the leopard was nearly on top of her. Then suddenly the animal noticed the switching tail and bolted like lightning, nearly over-running Nuru in its flight.

Elsa was now twenty-three months old and her voice broke to a deep growl. Now she began looking for a mate. Normally she followed us on our walks wherever we went, but for two days she had seemed determined to cross the valley. On this particular afternoon, she led us in *her* direction, and we soon found the fresh pugmarks of a lion. At dark, she refused to return. As we were near a car track, we went back to get the Land-Rover, and George set off in it while I stayed at home in case she took a short cut back. When he reached the place where we had left her, George shouted to her for some time, but there was no response – only the hills echoed his calls . . . He drove on for another mile, calling at intervals. Then, hoping that Elsa had already come home, he returned. I told him I had waited for two long hours, but that there was still no sign of her, so he left again and some time after he had gone I heard a shot. Until he came back I was very anxious, and then most upset by what he had to tell me.

He had driven out and called for a good half-hour, but Elsa had not shown up. Then he had stopped the car in an opening in the bush, wondering where to look next. Suddenly, some two hundred yards behind the car there had been a great uproar of lions quarrelling.

Then, the next moment a lioness flashed by with another in hot pursuit. As they shot past, George seized his rifle and put a bullet under the second animal, assuming, probably rightly, that she was a jealous lioness, bent on Elsa's destruction. Then he jumped into the car and gave chase. He drove along a narrow lane between dense thornbush, flashing a spotlight from side to side, until he was brought up short by a lion and two lionesses, who only very reluctantly moved out of his way, giving vent to loud roars.

Now he had come to fetch me; we drove back to the scene, but though we called desperately for Elsa – called and called – no familiar sound came in answer. But presently, as if in derision, the lion chorus started up a few hundred yards away. We drove towards them until we could see the glint of three pairs of eyes. There was nothing more to be done. So, with heavy hearts, we turned for home. Would Elsa be killed by a jealous lioness? However, to our great relief, we had not gone more than a mile along the track when we came upon Elsa, sniffing at a bush. She utterly ignored us. We tried to persuade her to join us but she remained where we had found her, gazing wistfully into the bush in the direction in which the lions had last been heard. Presently they started calling again, and approached. Thirty yards behind us was a dry river bed, and here the pride stopped, growling vigorously.

It was now well after midnight. Elsa sat in the moonlight between the lions and us; both parties called her to their side. Who was going to win the contest? Suddenly Elsa moved towards the lions and I shouted, 'Elsa, *no*, don't go there, you'll get killed.' She sat down again, looking at us and looking back at her own kind, undecided what to do. For an hour the situation did not alter, then George fired two shots over the lions; this had the effect of sending them off in silence. Then, as Elsa had still not made up her mind, we drove slowly back, hoping that she might follow us; and so she did. Very reluctantly, she walked parallel with the car, looking back many times, till finally she hopped on to the roof and we brought her back to safety. When we arrived home she was very thirsty and exhausted and drank without stopping.

What had happened during the five hours which Elsa had spent with the lions? Would a wild pride accept her in spite of the human smell which she carried? Why had she returned with us instead of joining her own kind? Was it because she was frightened of the fierce lioness? These were some of the questions we asked ourselves. The fact remained that she had come to no harm as a result of this experience.

But after this adventure the call of the wild evidently grew stronger and stronger. Often she did not return with us at dark and we spent many evenings looking for her. In the dry season water was our main hold on her, for this she could only get at the house.

Rocks were her favourite place, and she always chose the top of a cliff or some other safe position as her look-out. Once, in spite of hearing a leopard 'coughing' close by, we had to leave her on such a rock. Next morning she returned with several bleeding scratches and we wondered whether the leopard was responsible for them.

Another time, after sunset, she followed the laughing cries of a hyena; soon these increased to hysterical shrieks to which Elsa replied by loud growls. George rushed to see what was happening and was just in time to shoot one of two hyenas which were closing in on Elsa. After this she pulled her 'kill' into a bush, dragging it between her front legs as she had often done with a groundsheet when she was a cub. But, although she was now two years old, her teeth could not yet penetrate the skin of a hyena, and she did not know what to do with her quarry.

At this age giraffes still remained her favourite friends. She would stalk them, using every stratagem of her kind, but invariably they would spot her before she got too close; this was mainly because Elsa seemed unable to control her tail. Her body would freeze without so much as the twitch of an ear, but the conspicuous black tassel on her tail would never keep still. Once the giraffes had spotted her, there would be a competition to see who would be the boldest among them. One by one, in a half-circle, they would edge forward, giving vent to low, long-drawn snorts, until Elsa could contain herself no longer and would make a rush and put the herd to flight. On two occasions she made a sustained chase after a huge old bull; only after they had gone about a mile the giraffe, either winded or fed up with being chased, turned at bay. Elsa then circled him closely, keeping just out of reach of the mighty pounding forelegs, a blow from which could easily have smashed her skull.

Soon after her adventure with the lions Nuru reported that, when in the morning he tried to follow her, Elsa had growled at him repeatedly. Obviously she wished him to remain behind, while she walked determinedly into the hills. So, in spite of the increasing heat, she had trotted off quickly until he lost her tracks in the rocks. In the afternoon, we followed her spoor, but soon lost it and could only call to her from the foot of the cliffs. A reply came, a strange growl, unlike Elsa's voice but undoubtedly that of a lion. Soon afterwards we saw her struggling downhill, over the boulders, calling in her familiar way. When she reached us she flung herself exhausted on to the ground, panting and very excited. We had brought water with us and

she could not have enough of it. Now we noticed several bleeding claw marks on her hind legs, shoulders and neck and also two bleeding perforations on her forehead, which were definitely made by teeth and not by claws.

As soon as she had recovered a little, she greeted us in her customary manner, as well as purring at each of us in turn in a most startling way, as though to say, 'Listen to what I have learned.'

When she had assured herself of our admiration, she threw herself on the ground again and fell fast asleep for two hours. She had obviously just been with a lion when we had interfered by calling to her.

Two days later she spent a whole day and night away, and when we followed her spoor we found her in the company of a lioness; both having laid up several times together.

From this time onwards, Elsa spent more and more nights away. We tried to induce her to come home by driving near to her favourite places and calling to her. Occasionally she came, more often she did not. Sometimes she was away, without food or water, for two or three days. Water was still some hold over her, but soon the rains were due and we realised that when they came we should lose all control of her. This raised a problem which we had to solve; it was one which was

made more urgent by the fact that our long overseas leave was due in May. Elsa was now twenty-seven months old, almost full grown. We had always known that we could not keep her free indefinitely at Isiolo. Our original idea had been to send her to join her sisters at the Rotterdam Zoo, and we had even made the necessary arrangements in case an emergency should arise. But now she had taken her future into her own paws and her latest developments were decisive in altering our plans for her. Because we had been so fortunate in bringing her up in her natural environment and because she seemed so much at home in the bush and was accepted by wild animals, we felt that she might well prove to be the exception to the rule that a pet will be killed by its own kind because of its human smell and ignorance of bush life. To release Elsa back to the wild would be an experiment well worth trying.

We intended to spend two or three weeks with her. Then, if all went well, we would take our long leave.

Next we had to consider, *where* to release Elsa? Unfortunately Isiolo was far too populated for us to let her go wild there. But we knew of an area which for most of the year was devoid of inhabitants and livestock but had an abundance of game, especially lion.

We received permission to take Elsa to this place and made the necessary arrangements. The rains were expected any day, so we had no time to lose if she were to reach her possible future home before they began.

In order to get to this area we should have to travel three hundred and forty miles, crossing the highlands on our way and also the great rift valley, going through relatively thickly populated country where there were many European farms. Because we feared that Elsa might be embarrassed by gaping crowds and inquisitive Africans at every halt, and also to avoid the heat of the day, we decided to travel by night. We settled to start about seven in the evening, but Elsa had other ideas. Before setting off we took her out for her usual walk to her favourite rocks, across the valley from our house. There I photographed her for the last time in her home. She is genuinely camera-shy and always hates being filmed or sketched. As soon as she sees one of those awful shiny boxes focused on her she invariably turns her head, or covers it with a paw, or just walks away. On this day at Isiolo she had to endure a lot from our Leica and plainly got thoroughly fed up with it. So finally she took her revenge. When, for a moment, I left the camera unguarded, she leapt up, sprang upon it and galloped away with it over the rocks. That, we thought, was the end of our precious Leica. For more than an hour we tried every device to rescue it, but as we tried each new trick we had invented for the purpose, she shook it more provokingly between her teeth or chewed at it, holding it firmly between her paws. Finally we recovered it, and miraculously it was not badly damaged.

By then, it was time to get back to the house and start off on the long journey, but just then Elsa sat herself on a rock and gazed across the valley in the contemplative manner of her kind and nothing would move her. Obviously she had no intention of walking back and expected the car to be brought for her. All hope of making an early start was gone. George went home, fetched the car and came back to the foot of the hills where we had left Elsa, but she was no longer there and had apparently gone for her evening stroll. He called to her, but there was no response. Not until eleven at night did she reappear, jump on the roof of the Land-Rover and consent to be driven home.

It was after midnight when we had at last secured Elsa in her travelling crate and started off. In the hope of making the trip easier for her I gave her a tranquilliser; we had been told by the vet that the drug was harmless and that the effect would last about eight hours. To give Elsa all the moral support I could, I travelled with her in the open lorry. During the night we passed through country that is 8,000 feet above sea level, and the cold was icy. Owing to the effect of the tranquilliser Elsa was only semi-conscious, yet even in this state every few minutes she stretched her paws out throught the bars of the crate, to assure herself that I was still there. It took us seventeen hours to reach our destination. The effect of the tranquilliser did not wear off until an hour after we had arrived.

It was late in the afternoon by the time we reached our destination; there we were met by a friend who is the Game Warden of this district. We pitched camp on a superb site at the base of a thousand-foot escarpment overlooking a vast plain of open bush country, through which a belt of dark vegetation marks the course of a river. As we were at an altitude of 5,000 feet, the air was fresh and brisk. Immediately in front of our camp lay open grassland sloping towards the plain, on which herds of Thomson's gazelle, topi, wildebeeste, Burchell's zebra, roan antelope, kongoni, and a few buffalo were grazing. It was a game paradise. While the tents were being pitched we took Elsa for a stroll and she rushed at the herds, not knowing which to follow, for in every direction there were animals running. As if to shake off the effects of the ghastly journey, Elsa lost herself among these new playmates, who were rather astonished to find such a strange lion in their midst; one who rushed foolishly to and fro without any apparent purpose. Soon, however, Elsa had had enough and trotted back to camp and her dinner.

Our plan was this; we would spend the first week taking Elsa, perched on the roof of the Land-Rover, round the new country, thus getting her used to it and to the animals, many of which belonged to species which do not live in the Northern Frontier and she had therefore never seen. During the second week we intended to leave her overnight, while she was active in the bush, and to visit and feed her in the mornings when she was sleepy. Afterwards we would reduce her meals, in the hope that this would encourage her to kill on her own, or to join a wild lion.

On the morning after our arrival we started our programme. First we took off her collar, as the symbol of liberation. Elsa hopped on to the roof of the Land-Rover and we went off. After only a few hundred yards we saw a lioness walking parallel to us downhill. We drove closer to her. Elsa displayed much excitement, jumped off her seat and, making low moaning noises, cautiously followed this new friend. But as soon as the lioness stopped and turned round, her courage failed her and she raced back as fast as she could to the safety of the car. The lioness continued her purposeful walk, and we soon detected six cubs waiting for her on a small ant-hill in tall grass.

We drove on and surprised a hyena chewing a bone. Elsa jumped off and chased the startled animal, who had only time to grasp her bone and lumber away. In spite of her ungainliness, the hyena made good her escape but lost her bone in the process.

Later we passed through herd after herd of different antelope, whose curiosity seemed to be aroused by the sight of a Land-Rover with a lion on it and allowed us, provided that we remained in the car and did not talk, to approach within a few yards of them. All the time Elsa watched carefully, but did not attempt to leave the car unless she spotted an animal off guard, grazing with its back towards her, or fighting; then she would get down quietly and creep forward with her belly close to the ground, taking advantage of every bit of cover, and thus advance towards her victim. But as soon as the animal showed any suspicion, she either froze to immobility or, if the situation seemed better handled in another way, she pretended to be uninterested, licked her paws, yawned, or even rolled on her back, until the animal was reassured. Then she would at once start stalking again. But however cunning she was, she never got close enough to kill.

Joy Adamson

(1910–80)

Joy Adamson was one of those very energetic people who find almost everything of interest to them. She was a writer, sculptor, and studied metalworking and medicine. She was also a well-known book illustrator and artist and earned many awards for her paintings. Her favourite subjects were the people, animals and plant life of Kenya, where she lived. In 1956, Joy Adamson began to study wild animals and it was during this work that she, and her husband George, found Elsa the lioness.

CALL OF THE WILD

Buck is half St Bernard and half shepherd dog, a giant good-natured animal brought up in luxury in California. But it is the time of the Gold Rush in the Klondike and powerful dogs like Buck are in great demand. One day Buck is stolen and sold to be a sledge dog in the Yukon. He learns to survive in the pack but is harshly treated by one of his masters and is on the point of death when he is rescued by John Thornton.

When John Thornton froze his feet in the previous December, his partners had made him comfortable and left him to get well, going on themselves up the river to get out a raft of saw-logs for Dawson. He was still limping slightly at the time he rescued Buck, but with the continued warm weather even the slight limp left him. And here, lying by the river bank through the long spring days, watching the running water, listening lazily to the songs of birds and the hum of nature, Buck slowly won back his strength.

A rest comes very good after one has travelled three thousand miles, and it must be confessed that Buck waxed lazy as his wounds healed, his muscles swelled out, and the flesh came back to cover his bones. For that matter, they were all loafing – Buck, John Thornton, and Skeet and Nig – waiting for the raft to come that was to carry them down to Dawson. Skeet was a little Irish setter who early made friends with Buck, who, in a dying condition, was unable to resent her first advance. She had the doctor trait which some dogs possess; and as a mother cat washes her kittens, so she washed and cleansed Buck's wounds, Regularly, each morning, after he had finished his breakfast, she performed her self-appointed task, till he came to look for her ministrations as much as he did for Thornton's. Nig, equally friendly, though less demonstrative, was a huge black dog, half bloodhound and half deerhound, with eyes that laughed and a boundless good nature.

To Buck's surprise these dogs manifested no jealousy toward him. They seemed to share the kindliness and largeness of John Thornton. As Buck grew stronger they enticed him into all sorts of ridiculous games, in which Thornton himself could not forbear to join; and in this fashion Buck romped through his convalescence and into a new existence. Love, genuine passionate love, was his for the first time. This he had never experienced at Judge Miller's down in the sun-kissed Santa Clara Valley. With the Judge's son, hunting and tramping, it had been a working partnership; with the Judge's grandsons, a sort of pompous guardianship; and with the Judge himself, a stately and dignified friendship. But love that was feverish and burning, that was adoration, that was madness, it had taken John Thornton to arouse.

This man had saved his life, which was something; but, further, he was the ideal master. Other men saw to the welfare of their dogs from a sense of duty and business expediency; he saw to the welfare of his as if they were his own children, because he could not help it. And he saw further. He never forgot a kindly greeting or a cheering word, and to sit down for a long talk with them ('gas' he called it) was as much his delight as theirs. He had a way of taking Buck's head roughly between his hands, and resting his own head upon Buck's, of shaking him back and forth, the while calling him ill names that to Buck were love names. Buck knew no greater joy than that rough embrace and the sound of murmured oaths, and at each jerk back and forth it seemed that his heart would be shaken out of his body so great was its ecstasy. And when, released, he sprang to his feet, his mouth laughing, his eyes eloquent, his throat vibrant with unuttered sounds, and in that fashion remain without movement, John Thornton would reverently exclaim, 'God, you can all but speak!'

Buck had a trick of love expression that was akin to hurt. He would often seize Thornton's hand in his mouth and close so fiercely that the flesh bore impress of his teeth for some time afterward. And as Buck understood the oaths to be love words, so the man understood this feigned bite for a caress.

For the most part, however, Buck's love was expressed in adoration. While he went wild with happiness when Thornton touched him or spoke to him, he did not seek these tokens. Unlike Skeet, who was wont to shove her nose under Thornton's hand and nudge and nudge till petted, or Nig, who would stalk up and rest his great head on Thornton's knee, Buck was content to adore at a distance. He would lie by the hour, eager, alert, at Thornton's feet looking up into his face, dwelling upon it, studying it, following with keenest interest each fleeting expression, every movement or change of feature. Or, as chance might have it, he would lie farther away, to the side or rear, watching the outlines of the man and the occasional movements of his body. And often, such was the communion in which they lived, the strength of Buck's gaze would draw John Thornton's

head around, and he would return the gaze, without speech, his heart shining out of his eyes as Buck's heart shone out.

For a long time after his rescue, Buck did not like Thornton to get out of his sight. From the moment he left the tent to when he entered it again, Buck would follow at his heels. His transient masters since he had come into the Northland had bred in him a fear that no master could be permanent. He was afraid that Thornton would pass out of his life as Perrault and Françôis and the Scotch half-breed had passed out. Even in the night, in his dreams, he was haunted by this fear. At such times he would shake off sleep and creep through the chill to the flap of the tent, where he would stand and listen to the sound of his master's breathing.

But in spite of this great love he bore John Thornton, which seemed to bespeak the soft civilising influence, the strain of the primitive, which the Northland had aroused in him, remained alive and active.

Faithfulness and devotion, things born of fire and roof, were his, yet he retained his wildness and wiliness. He was a thing of the wild, come in from the wild to sit by John Thornton's fire, rather than a dog of the soft Southland stamped with the marks of generations of civilisation. Because of his very great love, he could not steal from this man, but from any man, in any other camp, he did not hesitate an instant; while the cunning with which he stole enabled him to escape detection.

His face and body were scored by the teeth of many dogs, and he fought as fiercely as ever and more shrewdly. Skeet and Nig were too good-natured for quarrelling – besides, they belonged to John Thornton; but the strange dog, no matter what the breed or valour, swiftly acknowledged Buck's supremacy or found himself struggling for life with a terrible antagonist. And Buck was merciless. He had learned well the law of club and fang, and he never forewent an advantage or drew back a foe he had started on the way to Death. He had lessoned from Spitz, and from the chief fighting dogs of the police and mail, and knew there was no middle course. He must master or be mastered; while to show mercy was a weakness. Mercy did not exist in the primordial life. It was misunderstood for fear, and such misunderstandings made for death. Kill or be killed, eat or be eaten, was the law; and this mandate, down out of the depths of Time, he obeyed.

He was older than the days he had seen and the breaths he had drawn. He linked the past with the present, and the eternity behind him throbbed through him in a mighty rhythm to which he swayed as the tides and seasons swayed. He sat by John Thornton's fire, a broad-breasted dog, white-fanged and long-furred; but behind him were the shades of all manner of dogs, half-wolves and wild wolves, urgent and prompting, tasting the savour of the meat he ate, thirsting for the water he drank, scenting the wind with him, listening with him and telling him the sounds made by the wild life in the forest, dictating his moods, directing his actions, lying down to sleep with him when he lay down, and dreaming with him and beyond him and becoming themselves the stuff of his dreams.

So peremptorily did these shades beckon him, that each day mankind and the claims of mankind slipped farther from him. Deep in the forest a call was sounding, and as often as he heard this call, mysteriously thrilling and luring, he felt compelled to turn his back upon the fire and the beaten earth around it, and to plunge into the forest, and on and on, he knew not where or why; nor did he wonder where or why, the call sounding imperiously, deep in the forest. But as

often as he gained the soft unbroken earth and the green shade, the love for John Thornton drew him back to the fire again.

Thornton alone held him. The rest of mankind was as nothing. Chance travellers might praise or pet him; but he was cold under it all, and from a too demonstrative man he would get up and walk away. When Thornton's partners, Hans and Pete, arrived on the long-expected raft Buck refused to notice them till he learned they were closet to Thornton; after that he tolerated them in a passive sort of way, accepting favours from them as though he favoured them by accepting. They were of the same large type as Thornton, living close to the earth, thinking simply and seeing clearly; and ere they swung the raft into the big eddy by the saw-mill at Dawson, they understood Buck and his ways, and did not insist upon an intimacy such as obtained with Skeet and Nig.

For Thornton, however, his love seemed to grow and grow. He,

alone among men, could put a pack upon Buck's back in the summer travelling. Nothing was too great for Buck to do, when Thornton commanded. One day (they had grub-staked themselves from the proceeds of the raft and left Dawson for the head-waters of the Tanana) the men and dogs were sitting on the crest of a cliff which fell away, straight down, to naked bed-rock three hundred feet below. John Thornton was sitting near the edge. Buck at his shoulder. A thoughtless whim seized Thornton, and he drew the attention of Hans and Pete to the experiment he had in mind. 'Jump, Buck!' he commanded, sweeping his arm out and over the chasm. The next instant he was grappling with Buck on the extreme edge, while Hans and Pete were dragging them back into safety.

'It's uncanny,' Pete said, after it was over and they had caught their speech.

Thornton shook his head. 'No, it is splendid, and it is terrible, too. Do you know, it sometimes makes me afraid.'

'I'm not hankering to be the man that lays hands on you while he's around,' Pete announced conclusively, nodding his head toward Buck.

'By Jingo!' was Hans' contribution. 'Not mineself either.'

It was at Circle City, 'ere the year was out, that Pete's apprehensions were realised. 'Black' Burton, a man evil-tempered and malicious, had been picking a quarrel with a tenderfoot at the bar, when Thornton stepped good-naturedly between. Buck, as was his custom, was lying in a corner, head on paws, watching his master's every action. Burton struck out, without warning, straight from the shoulder, Thornton was sent spinning, and saved himself from falling only by clutching the rail of the bar.

Those who were looking on heard what was neither bark nor yelp, but something which is best described as a roar, and they saw Buck's body rise up in the air as he left the floor for Burton's throat. The man saved his life by instinctively throwing out his arm, but was hurled backward to the floor with Buck on top of him. Buck loosed his teeth from the flesh of the arm and drove in again for the throat. This time the man succeeded only in partly blocking, and his throat was torn open. Then the crowd was upon Buck, and he was driven off; but while a surgeon checked the bleeding, he prowled up and down, growling furiously, attempting to rush in, and being forced back by an array of hostile clubs. A 'miners' meeting', called on the spot, decided that the dog had sufficient provocation, and Buck was discharged. but his reputation was made, and from that day his name spread through every camp in Alaska.

Later on, in the fall of the year, he saved John Thornton's life in quite another fashion. The three partners were lining a long and narrow poling-boat down a bad stretch of rapids on the Forty-Mile Creek. Hans and Pete moved along the bank, snubbing with a thin Manila rope from tree to tree, while Thornton remained in the boat, helping the descent by means of a pole, and shouting directions to the shore. Buck, on the bank, worried and anxious, kept abreast of the boat, his eyes never off his master.

At a particularly bad spot where a ledge of barely submerged rocks jutted out into the river, Hans cast off the rope, and, while Thornton poled the boat out into the stream, ran down the bank with the end in his hand to snub the boat when it had cleared the ledge. This it did, and was flying down-stream in a current as swift as a mill-race, when Hans checked it with his rope and checked it too suddenly. The boat flirted over and snubbed into the bank bottom up, while Thornton, flung sheer out of it, was carried down-stream towards the worst part of the rapids, a stretch of wild water in which no swimmer could live.

Buck had sprung in on the instant; and at the end of three hundred yards, amid a mad swirl of water, he overhauled Thornton. When he felt him grasp his tail, Buck headed for the bank, swimming with all his splendid strength. But the progress shoreward was slow; the progress down-stream amazingly rapid. From below came the fatal roaring where the wild current went wilder and was rent in shreds and spray by the rocks which thrust through like the teeth of an enormous comb. The suck of the water as it took the beginning of the last steep pitch was frightful, and Thornton knew that the shore was impossible. He scraped furiously over a rock, bruised across a second, and struck a third with crushing force. He clutched its slippery top with both hands, releasing Buck, and above the roar of the churning water shouted: 'Go, Buck! Go!'

Buck could not hold his own, and swept on downstream, struggling desperately, but unable to win back. When he heard Thornton's command repeated, he partly reared out of the water, throwing his head high as though for a last look, then turned obediently towards the bank. He swam powerfully and was dragged ashore by Pete and Hans at the very point where swimming ceased to be possible and destruction began.

They knew that the time a man could cling to a slippery rock in the face of that driving current was a matter of minutes, and they ran as fast as they could up the bank to a point far above where Thornton was hanging on. They attached the line with which they had been snubbing the boat to Buck's neck and shoulders, being careful that it should neither strangle him nor impede his swimming and launched him into the stream. He struck out boldly but not straight enough into the stream. He discovered the mistake too late, when Thornton was abreast of him and a bare half-dozen strokes away while he was being carried helplessly past.

Hans promptly snubbed with the rope, as though Buck were a boat. The rope thus tightening on him in the sweep of the current, he was jerked under the surface, and under the surface he remained till his body struck against the bank and he was hauled out. He was half drowned, and Hans and Pete threw themselves upon him, pounding the breath into him and the water out of him. He staggered to his feet and fell down. The faint sound of Thornton's voice came to them, and though they could not make out the words of it, they knew that he was in his extremity. His master's voice acted on Buck like an electric shock. He sprang to his feet and ran up the bank ahead of the men to the point of his previous departure.

Jack London

(1876–1916)

The American writer, Jack London, had a very adventurous life. When he was 17, in 1893, he became a seaman and went on a voyage to Japan and Siberia. Afterwards, he worked as a journalist. Then, at 18, he journeyed on foot through the USA and Canada. By the time he was 21, Jack London had dug for gold in the Klondyke region of Canada, and then decided to become a full-time writer. As a newspaper correspondent, he reported on the war between Russia and Japan in 1904/5.

MOBY DICK

Captain Ahab, the harsh and bitter master of the whaling ship Pequod *holds Moby Dick, the giant white whale, responsible for the loss of his leg and is determined to seek revenge. One night, the creature is spotted and the* Pequod *embarks on an exciting chase which all the crew know will end in the destruction of either Ahab or Moby Dick.*

THAT NIGHT, in the mid-watch, when the old man – as his wont at intervals – stepped forth from the scuttle in which he leaned, and went to his pivot-hole, he suddenly thrust out his face fiercely, snuffing up the sea air as a sagacious ship's dog will, in drawing nigh to some barbarous isle. He declared that a whale must be near. Soon that peculiar odour, sometimes to a great distance given forth by the living Sperm Whale, was palpable to all the watch; nor was any mariner surprised when, after inspecting the compass, and then the dog-vane, and then ascertaining the precise bearing of the odour as nearly as possible, Ahab rapidly ordered the ship's course to be slightly altered, and the sail to be shortened.

The acute policy dictating these movements was sufficiently vindicated at daybreak by the sight of a long sleek on the sea directly and lengthwise ahead, smooth as oil, and resembling in the pleated watery wrinkles bordering it, the polished metallic-like marks of some swift tide-rip, at the mouth of a deep, rapid stream.

'Man the mastheads! Call all hands!'

Thundering with the butts of three clubbed handspikes on the forecastle deck, Daggoo roused the sleepers with such judgment claps that they seemed to exhale from the scuttle, so intantaneously did they appear with their clothes in their hands.

'What d'ye see?' cried Ahab, flattening his face to the sky.

'Nothing, nothing, sir!' was the sound hailing down in reply.

'T'gallant-sails! stunsails alow and aloft, and on both sides!'

All sail being set, he now cast loose the life-line, reserved for swaying him to the mainroyal masthead; and in a few moments they were hoisting him thither, when, while but two-thirds of the way aloft, and while peering ahead through the horizontal vacancy between the maintopsail and top-gallant-sail, he raised a gull-like cry in the air, 'There she blows! – there she blows! A hump like a snowhill! It is Moby Dick!'

Fired by the cry which seemed simultaneously taken up by the three lookouts, the men on deck rushed to the rigging to behold the famous whale they had so long been pursuing. Ahab had now gained his final perch, some feet above the other lookouts. Tashtego standing just beneath him on the cap of the top-gallant-mast, so that the Indian's head was almost on a level with Ahab's heel. From this

height the whale was now seen some mile or so ahead, at every roll of the sea revealing his high sparkling hump, and regularly jetting his silent spout into the air. To the credulous mariners it seemed the same silent spout they had so long ago beheld in the moonlit Atlantic and Indian Oceans.

'And did none of ye see it before?' cried Ahab, hailing the perched men all around him.

'I saw him almost that same instant, sir, that Captain Ahab did, and I cried out,' said Tashtego.

'Not the same instant; not the same – no, the doubloon is mine, Fate reserved the doubloon for me. *I* only; none of ye could have raised the White Whale first. There she blows! there she blows! – there she blows! There again! – there again!' he cried, in long-drawn, lingering, methodic tones, attuned to the gradual prolongings of the whale's visible jets. 'He's going to sound! In stunsails! Down top-gallant-sails! stand by three boats. Mr Starbuck, remember, stay on board, and keep the ship. Helm there! Luff, luff a point! So; steady, man, steady! There go flukes! No, no; only black water! All ready the boats there? Stand by, stand by! Lower me, Mr Starbuck; lower, lower – quick, quicker!' and he slid through the air to the deck.

'He is heading straight to leeward, sir,' cried Stubb; 'right away from us; cannot have seen the ship yet.'

'Be dumb, man! Stand by the braces! Hard down the helm! – brace up! Shiver her! – shiver her! So; well that! Boats, boats!'

Soon all the boats but Starbuck's were dropped; all the boat-sails set – all the paddles plying; with rippling swiftness, shooting to

leeward; and Ahab heading the onset. A pale, death-glimmer lit up Fedallah's sunken eyes; a hideous motion gnawed his mouth.

Like noiseless nautilus shells, their light prows sped through the sea; but only slowly they neared the foe. As they neared him, the ocean grew still more smooth; seemed drawing a carpet over its waves; seemed a noon-meadow, so serenely it spread. At length the breathless hunter came so nigh his seemingly unsuspecting prey, that his entire dazzling hump was distinctly visible, sliding along the sea as if an isolated thing, and continually set in a revolving ring of finest, fleecy, greenish foam. He saw the vast involved wrinkles of the slightly projecting head behind. Before it, far out on the soft Turkish-rugged waters, went the glistening white shadow from his broad, milky forehead, a musical rippling playfully accompanying the shade; and behind, the blue waters interchangeably flowed over into the moving valley of his steady wake; and on either hand bright bubbles arose and danced by his side. But these were broken again by the light toes of hundreds of gay fowl softly feathering the sea, alternate with their fitful flight; and like to some flagstaff rising from the painted hull of an argosy, the tall but shattered pole of a recent lance projected from the white whale's back; and at intervals one of the cloud of soft-toed fowls hovering, and to and fro skimming like a canopy over the fish, silently perched and rocked on this pole, the long tail feathers streaming like pennons.

A gentle joyousness a mighty mildness of repose in swiftness, invested the gliding whale. Not the white bull Jupiter swimming away with ravished Europa clinging to his graceful horns; his lovely, leering eyes sideways intent upon the maid; with smooth bewitching fleetness, rippling straight for the nuptial bower in Crete; not Jove did surpass the glorified White Whale as he so divinely swam.

On each soft side – coincident with the parted swell, that but once laving him, then flowed so wide away – on each bright side, the whale shed off enticings. No wonder there had been some among the hunters who namelessly transported and allured by all this serenity, had ventured to assail it; but had fatally found that quietude but the vesture of tornadoes. Yet calm, enticing calm, oh, whale! thou glidest on, to all who for the first time eye thee, no matter how many in that same way thou may'st have bejuggled and destroyed before.

And thus, through the serene tranquillities of the tropical sea, among waves whose hand-clappings were suspended by exceeding rapture, Moby Dick moved on, still withholding from sight the full terrors of his submerged trunk, entirely hiding the wretched hideousness of his jaw. But soon the fore part of him slowly rose from the water; for an instant his whole marbleised body formed a high arch, like Virginia's Natural Bridge, and warmingly waving his bannered flukes in the air, the grand god revealed himself, sounded, and went out of sight. Hoveringly halting, and dipping on the wing, the white sea-fowls longingly lingered over the agitated pool that he left.

With oars apeak, and paddles down, the sheets of their sails adrift, the three boats now stilly floated, awaiting Moby Dick's reappearance.

'Ah, hour,' said Ahab, standing rooted in his boat's stern, and he gazed beyond the whale's place, towards the dim blue spaces and wide wooing vacancies to leeward. It was only an instant; for again his eyes seemed whirling round in his head as he swept the watery circle. The breeze now freshened; the sea began to swell.

'The birds! – the birds!' cried Tashtego.

In long Indian file, as when herons take wing, the white birds were now all flying towards Ahab's boat; and when within a few yards began fluttering over the water there, wheeling round and round, with joyous, expectant cries. Their vision was keener than man's; Ahab could discover no sign in the sea. But suddenly as he peered down and down into its depths, he profoundly saw a white living spot no bigger than a white weasel, with wonderful celerity uprising, and magnifying as it rose, till it turned, and then there were plainly revealed two long crooked rows of white, glistening teeth, floating up from the undiscoverable bottom. It was Moby Dick's open mouth and scrolled jaw; his vast, shadowed bulk still half blending with the blue of the sea. The glittering mouth yawned beneath the boat like an open-doored marble tomb; and giving one sidelong sweep with his steering oar, Ahab whirled the craft aside from this tremendous apparition. Then, calling upon Fedallah to change places with him, went forward to the bows, and seizing Perth's harpoon, commanded his crew to grasp their oars and stand by to stern.

Now, by reason of this timely spinning round the boat upon its axis, its bow, by anticipation, was made to face the whale's head while yet under water. But as if perceiving this stratagem, Moby Dick, with that malicious intelligence ascribed to him, sidelingly transplanted himself, as it were, in an instant, shooting his plaited head lengthwise beneath the boat.

Through and through; through every plank and each rib, it thrilled for an instant, the whale obliquely lying on his back, in the manner of a biting shark, slowly and feelingly taking its bows full within his mouth, so that the long, narrow, scrolled lower jaw curled high up into the open air, and one of the teeth caught in a rowlock. The bluish pearl-white of the inside of the jaw was within six inches of Ahab's head, and reached higher than that. In this attitude the White Whale now shook the slight cedar as a mildly cruel cat her mouse. With unastonished eyes Fedallah gazed, and crossed his arms; but the tiger-yellow crew were tumbling over each other's heads to gain the uttermost stern.

And now, while both elastic gunwales were springing in and out, as the whale dallied with the doomed craft in this devilish way; and from his body being submerged beneath the boat, he could not be darted at from the bows, for the bows were almost inside of him, as it were; and while the other boats involuntarily paused, as before a quick crisis impossible to withstand, then it was that monomaniac Ahab, furious with this tantalising vicinity of his foe, which placed him all alive and helpless in the very jaws he hated; frenzied with all this, he seized the long bone with his naked hands, and wildly strove to wrench it from its gripe. As now he thus vainly strove, the jaw slipped from him; the frail gunwales bent in, collapsed, and snapped, as both jaws, like an enormous shears, sliding further aft, bit the craft completely in twain, and locked themselves fast again in the sea, midway between the two floating wrecks. These floated aside, the

broken ends drooping, the crew at the stern-wreck clinging to the gunwales, and striving to hold fast to the oars to lash them across.

At that preluding moment, ere the boat was yet snapped, Ahab, the first to preceive the whale's intent, by the crafty upraising of his head, a movement that loosed his hold for the time; at that moment his hand had made one final effort to push the boat out of the bite. But only slipping further into the whale's mouth, and tilting over sideways as it slipped, the boat had shaken off his hold on the jaw; spilled him out of it, as he leaned to the push; and so he fell flat-faced upon the sea.

Ripplingly withdrawing from his prey, Moby Dick now lay at a little distance, vertically thrusting his oblong white head up and down in the billows; and at the same time slowly revolving his whole spindled body; so that when his vast wrinkled forehead rose – some twenty or more feet out of the water – the now rising swells, with all their confluent waves, dazzling broke against it; vindictively tossing their shivered spray still higher into the air. So, in a gale, the but half baffled Channel billows only recoil from the base of the Eddystone, triumphantly to overleap its summit with their scud.

But soon resuming his horizontal attitude, Moby Dick swam swiftly round and round the wrecked crew; sideways churning the water in his vengeful wake, as if lashing himself up to still another and more deadly assault. The sight of the splintered boat seemed to madden him, as the blood of grapes and mulberries cast before Antiochus's elephants in the book of Maccabees. Meanwhile Ahab half smothered in the foam of the whale's insolent tail, and too much of a cripple to swim, – though he could still keep afloat, even in the heart of such a whirlpool as that; helpless Ahab's head was seen, like a tossed bubble which the least chance shock might burst. From the boat's fragmentary stern, Fedallah incuriously and mildly eyed him;

the clinging crew, at the other drifting end, could not succour him; more than enough was it for them to look to themselves. For so revolvingly appalling was the White Whale's aspect, and so planetarily swift the ever-contracting circles he made, that he seemed horizontally swooping upon them. And though the other boats, unharmed, still hovered hard by, still they dared not pull into the eddy to strike, lest that should be the signal for the instant destruction of the jeopardised castaways, Ahab and all; nor in that case could they themselves hope to escape. With straining eyes, then, they remained on the outer edge of the direful zone, whose centre had now become the old man's head.

Meanwhile, from the beginning all this had been descried from the ship's mastheads; and squaring her yards, she had borne down upon the scene; and was now so nigh, that Ahab in the water hailed her; – 'Sail on the' – but that moment a breaking sea dashed on him from Moby Dick, and whelmed him for the time. But struggling out of it again, and chancing to rise on a towering crest, he shouted, – 'Sail on the whale! – Drive him off!'

The *Pequod*'s prows were pointed; and breaking up the charmed circle, she effectually parted the White Whale from his victim. As he sullenly swam off, the boats flew to the rescue.

Dragged into Stubb's boat with bloodshot, blinded eyes, the white brine caking in his wrinkles; the long tension of Ahab's bodily strength did crack, and helplessly he yielded to his body's doom: for a time, lying all crushed in the bottom of Stubb's boat, like one trodden under foot of herds of elephants. Far inland, nameless wails came from him, as desolate sounds from out ravines.

But this intensity of his physical prostration did but so much the more abbreviate it. In an instant's compass, great hearts sometimes condense to one deep pang, the sum-total of those shallow pains kindly diffused through feebler men's whole lives. And so, such hearts, though summary in each one suffering; still, if the gods decree it, in their lifetime aggregate a whole age of woe, wholly made up of instantaneous intensities; for even in their pointless centres, those noble natures contain the entire circumferences of inferior souls.

'The harpoon,' said Ahab, half-way rising, and draggingly leaning on one bended arm – 'is it safe?'

'Aye, sir, for it was not darted; this is it,' said Stubb, showing it.

'Lay it before me; – any missing men?'

'One, two, three, four, five; – there were five oars, sir, and here are five men.'

'That's good. – Help me, man; I wish to stand. So, so, I see him! there! there! going to leeward still; what a leaping spout! Hands off from me! The eternal sap runs up in Ahab's bones again! Set the sail; out oars; the helm!'

It is often the case that when a boat is stove, its crew, being picked up by another boat, help to work that second boat; and the chase is thus continued with what is called double-banked oars. It was thus now. But the added power of the boat did not equal the added power of the whale, for he seemed to have treble-banked his every fin; swimming with a velocity which plainly showed, that if now, under these circumstances, pushed on, the chase would prove an indefinitely prolonged, if not a hopeless one; nor could any crew endure for so long a period, such an unintermitted, intense, straining at the oar; a thing barely tolerable only in some one brief vicissitude. The ship itself, then, as it sometimes happens, offered the most promising intermediate means of overtaking the chase. Accordingly, the boats now made for her, and were soon swayed up to their cranes – the two parts of the wrecked boat having been previously secured by her – and then hoisting everything to her side, and stacking her canvas high up, and sideways outstretching it with stunsails, like the double-jointed wings of an albatross; the *Pequod* bore down in the leeward wake of Moby Dick. At the well-known, methodic intervals, the whale's glittering spout was regularly announced from the manned mastheads; and when he would be reported as just gone down, Ahab would take the time, and then pacing the deck, binnacle-watch in hand, so soon as the last second of the allotted hour expired, his voice was heard. – 'Whose is the doubloon now? D'ye see him?' and if the reply was, 'No, sir!' straightway he commanded them to lift him to his perch. In this way the day wore on; Ahab, now aloft and motionless; anon, unrestingly pacing the planks.

As he was thus walking, uttering no sound, except to hail the men aloft, or to bid them hoist a sail still higher, or to spread one to a still greater breadth – thus to and fro pacing, beneath his slouched hat, at every turn he passed his own wrecked boat, which had been dropped upon the quarter-deck, and lay there reversed; broken bow to shattered stern. At last he paused before it; and as in an already over-clouded sky fresh troops of clouds will sometimes sail across, so over the old man's face there now stole some such added gloom as this.

Stubb saw him pause; and perhaps intending, not vainly, though, to evince his own unabated fortitude, and this keep up a valiant place in his Captain's mind, he advanced, and eyeing the wreck exclaimed – 'This thistle the ass refused; it pricked his mouth too keenly, sir; ha! ha!'

'What soulless thing is this that laughs before a wreck? Man, man! did I not know thee brave as fearless fire (and as mechanical) I could swear thou wert a poltroon. Groan nor laugh should be heard before a wreck.'

'Aye, sir,' said Starbuck, drawing near, ''tis a solemn sight; an omen, and an ill one.'

'Omen? omen? – the dictionary! If the gods think to speak outright to man, they will honourably speak outright; not shake their heads, and give an old wife's darkling hint. – Begone! Ye two are the opposite poles of one thing; Starbuck is Stubb reversed, and Stubb is Starbuck; and ye two are all mankind; and Ahab stands alone among the millions of the peopled earth, nor gods nor men his neighbours! Cold, cold – I shiver! – How now? Aloft there! D'ye see him? Sing out for every spout, though he spout ten times a second!'

The day was nearly done; only the hem of his golden robe was rustling. Soon, it was almost dark, but the look-out men still remained unset.

'Can't see the spout now, sir; – too dark' – cried a voice from the air.

'How heading when last seen?'

'As before, sir, – straight to leeward.'

'Good! he will travel slower now 'tis night. Down royals and top-gallant stunsails, Mr Starbuck. We must not run over him before morning; he's making a passage now, and may heave-to a while. Helm there! keep her full before the wind! – Aloft come down! – Mr Stubb, send a fresh hand to the foremast head, and see it manned till morning.' – Then advancing towards the doubloon in the mainmast – 'Men, this gold is mine, for I earned it; but I shall let it abide here till the White Whale is dead; and then, whosoever of ye first raises him, upon the day he shall be killed, this gold is that man's; and if on that day I shall again raise him, then, ten times its sum shall be divided among all of ye! Away now! – the deck is thine, sir.'

And so saying, he placed himself half-way within the scuttle, and slouching his hat, stood there till dawn, except when at intervals rousing himself to see how the night wore on.

Herman Melville

(1819–91)

Herman Melville's life, like Jack London's, was very eventful and full of excitement. Born in New York, Melville made several sea voyages, including two on whaling ships. There, he saw for himself the hard, dangerous life led by whale-hunters. During his career as a sailor, Melville was once captured by a tribe who were said to be cannibals. Melville used his adventures in his novels, including Moby Dick, *his sixth book, and perhaps one of the greatest sea-stories ever written.*

Acknowledgements

By arrangement with publishers, authors and other owners of copyright, permissions have been granted to publish extracts included in this book. The publishers have made every attempt to trace copyright holders. If we have inadvertently omitted to acknowledge anyone, we should be most grateful if this could be brought to our attention for correction at the first opportunity. The publishers are most grateful to the following for their courtesy and co-operation:

Born Free, by Joy Adamson. Copyright © 1960 Joy Adamson. Reprinted by permission of Pantheon Books, a division of Random House Inc. and to William Collins Sons and Co Ltd.

The New Noah by Gerald Durrell. Reprinted by permission of Curtis Brown Ltd on behalf of Gerald Durrell. Copyright © Gerald Durrell 1955, published by Collins.

The Horse and His Boy Copyright © C S Lewis 1954 published by Collins.

The Mouse Butcher by Dick King-Smith. Copyright © Dick King-Smith 1981. Reprinted by permission of Victor Gollancz Ltd and Viking Penguin Inc.

Charlotte's Web by E B White. Reprinted by permission of Hamish Hamilton Ltd and Harper and Row Inc.

A Kestrel for a Knave by Barry Hines. Copyright © Barry Hines 1968. Reprinted by permission of Michael Joseph Ltd and Curtis Brown Ltd.

Ring of Bright Water by Gavin Maxwell. Copyright © Gavin Maxwell 1960 (Penguin Books 1974) Reprinted by permission of Penguin Books Ltd and by E P Dutton, a division of NAL Penguin Inc.

Thomasina by Paul Gallico. Courtesy of Mathemata Anstalt AG.

Photo Acknowledgements

The publishers would like to thank the following organisations and photographers for their kind permission to reproduce their photographs in this book:

BBC Hulton Picture Library 90; Campbell, Thompson & McLaughlin 41; Collins 131; Curtis Brown 120; Victor Gollancz Ltd/Michael Dyer 112; Harper & Row/Donald E Johnson 65; Michael Joseph Ltd 26: Keystone Collection 155; Popperfoto 141; Universal Pictorial Press 53.